From Intelligent t

MW01174869

The concept of smart cities offers a revolutionary vision of urban design for sustainability. Utilising the intelligent application of new technologies, smart cities also incorporate considerations of social and environmental capital in order to transform the life and work of cities.

This book brings together papers from leading international experts on the transition to smart cities. Drawing upon the experiences of cities in the USA, Canada and Europe, the authors describe the definitional components, critical insights and institutional means by which we can achieve truly smart cities. The resulting volume will be of interest to all involved in urban planning, architecture and engineering, as well as all interested in urban sustainability.

This book was originally published as a special issue of *Intelligent Buildings International*.

Mark Deakin is Professor of Built Environment at Edinburgh Napier University, UK.

Husam Al Waer is Lecturer in Sustainable Architecture and Urban Development at the University of Dundee, UK.

These essays set the foundation for new thinking about intelligent cities and how smart they can be for individual citizens and communities. The style is international, well argued and leads the way by taking a holistic approach to the planning and design of cities.

Derek Clements-Croome, Editor of Intelligent Buildings International

I find it very refreshing that these articles are focussing on one of the most important and foremost subjects in the built environment design field. They ask the question of what smart cities are, and how may they be formulated and arranged to ensure cities remain functional both for today and future generations.

Matt Kitson, Director of Sustainability, Hilson Moran

At a time when transnational corporations such as IBM are re-configuring themselves into expediters of a "Smart Planet", and are spending millions of dollars in advertising to brand themselves purveyors of "Smart Cities", it is important to have disinterested observers analyze the terms and realities of these campaigns. The Deakin and Al Waer (book) accomplishes this nicely. (The book) will continue to be relevant because (it contains) seminal contributions to discussions that will be occurring for a long time.

Richard E. Hanley, Editor of the Journal of Urban Technology

From Intelligent to Smart Cities

Edited by
Mark Deakin and Husam Al Waer

Routledge
Taylor & Francis Group

LONDON AND NEW YORK

First published 2012
by Routledge
2 Park Square, Milton Park, Abingdon, Oxfordshire OX14 4RN

Simultaneously published in the USA and Canada
by Routledge
711 Third Avenue, New York, NY 10017

First issued in paperback 2014

Routledge is an imprint of the Taylor and Francis Group, an informa business

© 2012 Taylor & Francis

This book is a reproduction of *Intelligent Buildings International*, vol. 3, issue 3. The Publisher requests to those authors who may be citing this book to state, also, the bibliographical details of the special issue on which the book was based.

All rights reserved. No part of this book may be reprinted or reproduced or utilised in any form or by any electronic, mechanical, or other means, now known or hereafter invented, including photocopying and recording, or in any information storage or retrieval system, without permission in writing from the publishers.

Trademark notice: Product or corporate names may be trademarks or registered trademarks, and are used only for identification and explanation without intent to infringe.

British Library Cataloguing in Publication Data
A catalogue record for this book is available from the British Library

ISBN13: 978-1-84971-389-4 (hbk)
ISBN13: 978-0-415-75489-7 (pbk)

Typeset in Times New Roman
by Taylor & Francis Books

Publisher's Note
The publisher would like to make readers aware that the chapters in this book may be referred to as articles as they are identical to the articles published in the special issue. The publisher accepts responsibility for any inconsistencies that may have arisen in the course of preparing this volume for print.

Contents

Introduction
From intelligent to smart cities

Mark Deakin[1], and Husam Al Waer[2]

[1]School of Engineering & Built Environment, Edinburgh Napier University, Merchiston Campus, 10 Colinton Road, Edinburgh EH10 5DT, UK
[2]School of Architecture, University of Dundee, Dundee, Scotland DD1 5EH, UK

Drawing upon the smart experiences of 'world class' cities in N. America, Canada and Europe, this special issue draws together five papers from leading international experts on the transition from intelligent to smart cities. Together they do what Hollands ('Will the real smart city stand up?' *City* 12(3), 302–320) has recently asked of smart cities and provide the definitional components, critical insights and institutional means by which to get beyond the all-too-often self-congratulatory tone cities across the world strike when claiming to be smart.

The first paper, from Deakin and Al Waer, reflects upon some of the anxieties surrounding the transition from intelligent to smart cities. In particular, it considers the anxiety that the transition has more to do with cities meeting the needs of the market, than the intelligence which is required for them to be smart. Working on the assumption that any attempt to overcome such an anxiety means shifting attention away from the needs of the market and towards the intelligence which is required for cities to be smart, this paper begins to set out a less presumptuous, more critically aware and insightful understanding of the transition. This less presumptuous, more critically aware and insightful understanding of the transition leads to the realization that it is the legacy of Castells (1996) and Graham and Marvin's (1996, 2001) work undertaken on the informational basis of the communications embedded in such intelligence, rather than Mitchell's (1995, 1999, 2001, 2003), which leads us away from the purely technical issues surrounding the business logic of such developments. That is to say, away from the purely technical aspects of such developments and towards an examination of the social capital which is not only critical in underpinning their informational and communicative qualities, but pivotal in supporting the wider environmental and cultural role intelligence plays in supporting the transition to smart cities.

What follows captures the information-rich and highly communicative qualities of these technical, social, wider environmental and cultural developments, the particular methodological issues they pose and the critically insightful role which the networks of innovation and creative partnerships set up to embed such intelligence play in the learning, knowledge transfer and capacity-building exercises that service the transition to smart cities. This is what the paper suggests

Hollands' (2008) account of smart cities misses and it goes some way to explain why he asks 'the real smart city to stand up!' For, in cutting across the legacy of the transition from the informational to the intelligent and now smart city, Hollands' (2008) account of the transition is not as well grounded in the informational and communicative qualities of the embedded intelligence they are built on.

This, the paper suggests, is a critical insight of some note, for only in giving such a well-grounded account of the embedded intelligence drawn attention to does it become possible to do what Hollands (2008) asks of smart cities: that is 'undergird' the social capital which is not only critical in underpinning the informational and communicative qualities of the embedded intelligence smart cities stand on, but pivotal in gaining a fuller insight into their significance.

The second paper, from Paskaleva, suggests that, over the course of the past decade, the smart cities agenda is an issue that has gained real momentum in Europe. The significance of this is reinforced further by other international organizations, such as the Organisation for Economic Cooperation and Development, who suggest that smart cities offer society the prospect of being not only environmentally sustainable, but also sufficiently competitive and cohesive to meet their emerging quality-of-life agenda (OECD – EUROSTAT, 2005). As the paper points out, as a result of such high-ranking institutional support, many cities have now adopted this socially cohesive, environmentally sound and economically competitive reading of what it means to be smart, as a way of profiling themselves as forward-looking, prosperous and well endowed. For instance:

- the Amsterdam Smart City initiative emphasizes the importance of collaboration between the citizens, government and businesses to develop smart projects that will 'change the world' by saving energy;

- Southampton City Council uses smart cards to stress the importance of integrated e-services;
- the City of Edinburgh Council has formed a smart city vision around an action plan for government transformation;
- the Malta Smart City strategy promotes a business park as a way to leverage economic growth;
- IBM, Siemens and ORACLE have formed their visions of the Smart Planet;
- a number of EU research and policy projects have emerged as well to deal with various issues of the 'smart city' (Komninos, 2002, 2008). The recently concluded pan-European research project IntelCities, for example, concluded that governance, as a process and outcome of joint decision making, has a leading role to play in building the 'smart city' and that cities should develop collaborative digital environments to boost local competitiveness and prosperity by using knowledge networks as a means to integrate the governance of e-service delivery (Curwell et al., 2005; Deakin and Allwinkle, 2007; Paskaleva, 2009);[1]
- the Smart Cities INTERREG project is also using an innovation network between academic, industrial and governmental partners to develop the 'triple helix' of e-services in the North Sea Region by way of and through a novel customization process (Deakin, 2010).

Paskaleva's paper advocates this view of smarter cities as people-based, human and progressive in their deployment of digital technologies, not to hardwire themselves, but instead to be socially inclusive in using them to foster good governance and create services capable of improving the quality of life.

Taking this 'digitally inclusive' vision of cities (Deakin, 2007, 2011) forward, the paper reflects upon the current trends and understanding of what it means for urban administrations, policy makers and businesses in Europe to be smart, and what it takes for them to become smarter. In developing this vision, the paper pays particular attention to the role of the 'smart city' as a nexus for open innovation and how the strategic significance of this development has become the mainstay of current discussions about the future of the Internet, living labs, innovation and competitiveness-driven (urban) development.

By conducting a critical review of some high-profile programmes and initiatives on smart cities, the emerging trends are explored and insights are drawn about the challenges these developments pose. The analysis is based on four Smart City projects and their relevant EU programmes. They are chosen because, collectively, they reveal what Europe expects smart cities to stand for.

Set within the terms of reference set out by Paskaleva, the paper from Komninos discusses the spatial intelligence of (smart) cities, the use of digital technologies and the institutional settings of those innovation systems seen as smart enough to radically transform cities. The paper has as its starting point two related observations about the increased use of terms like intelligent and smart in contemporary urban planning and development. The first concerns the somewhat over-simplistic way cities tend to use the term 'intelligent', or 'smart'. The second relates to the diverse range of strategies cities are currently assembling in laying claim to such a status. The observation here is that such a diverse range of strategies tends to say more about the ambiguity of the relationship digital technologies have to the planning and development of cities, rather than what it means for them to be ether intelligent, or smart. This is because, for Komninos, the strategies in question are seen as being left with plans insufficiently developed for their digital technologies to either embed the intelligence needed for cities to be smart, or build the means required for them to claim such status.

As a counterpoise to these observations, this paper lays down some of the 'fundamentals of spatial intelligence', the strategies and applications of which can be seen as being smart. It argues that, despite the great diversity of strategies and applications, the logistics of spatial intelligence teaches us that smart cities rest on a few knowledge-based trajectories. In particular, they rest on those knowledge-based trajectories that are embedded in the transitions of Bletchley Park, Hong Kong and Amsterdam and which the paper suggests are still only partially understood.

Taking Komninos' idea that cities are still stuck in the digital, rather than embedded in the intelligence of what is smart, as the 'third' observation on the transition, the paper from Deakin examines the thesis on the 'embedded intelligence of smart cities' first advanced by Mitchell (1995, 1999, 2003). For, as the paper points out, while Mitchell (1995) sets out a vision of urban life literally done to bits, left fragmented and in danger of coming unstuck, Mitchell's (1999) e-*topia* offers a counter-point to this and an image of the city no longer left in bits, but a place 'where it all comes together'.

Dwelling on the reconciliatory nature of these statements, this paper suggests that, while this thesis on the 'coming together' of the virtual and physical and dissolution of the boundaries between 'cyber and meat space' is compelling, there are a number of concerns surrounding the technical, social and environmental status of the embedded intelligence which is currently available for urban planners and developers to make cities smart. While problematic in itself, the paper also suggests that if the difficulties experienced over the transition from intelligent to smart cities were only methodological they might perhaps be manageable, but the problem is that they run deeper than this and relate to more substantive issues which surround the trajectory of Mitchell's (1995, 1999, 2003) thesis.

This, the paper suggests, is a critical insight of some significance because, if the trajectory of the thesis is not in the direction of either the embedded intelligence of smart cities, or the ICTs of what is referred to as 'digitally inclusive regeneration platforms', then the question arises as to whether the whole notion of e-topia can be seen as a progressive force for change, or merely as a way for the embedded intelligence of smart cities to reproduce the status quo.

This unfortunate scenario is drawn from what Graham and Marvin (1996, 2001) have referred to, not as e-topia, but splintering urbanism, because, under their thesis, the citizenship underlying the informatics of these communities is no longer able to carry the sheer weight of the material which such a cybernetic-based networking of intelligence is supposed to support. This, the paper suggests, is important because such a representation of the transition offers what can only be referred to as the antithesis to Mitchell's (1999) e-topia. An antithesis that, it might well be added, goes to some length to search out, uncover and expose the other side of this cybernetic-based intelligence and reveal what currently lies hidden in the debate which is currently taking place about the transition to smart cities.

From this perspective, the paper suggests the problems with e-topia are as much substantive as methodological, the former holding the key to the latter. In substantive terms this paper offers another twist on the question as to what the transition from intelligent to smart cities means and, in doing so, goes very much against the grain, arguing that our current understanding of embedded intelligence, smart cities and the ICTs of digitally inclusive regeneration puts us on the verge of a new environmental determinism.

To avoid repeating this mistake (yet) again, attention is drawn to the work of Graham and Marvin (1996, 2001) and the spaces which their radical democratic, i.e. egalitarian and ecologically integral, account of the transition opens up for a much more emancipatory view of the intelligence embedded in those knowledge-based agents smart enough to meet these requirements. Those knowledge-based agents, it should perhaps be added, who are smart enough to meet these requirements and do so by way of and through their exploitation of the social capital that

underlies the very communities which give rise to the norms, rules and values of such developments.

The paper suggests that, in ignoring these warnings and being unable to learn the lessons which such a critical reworking of the thesis offers, the strategy Mitchell (1999, 2003) adopts must be seen as suspect. Not only because the vision and scenarios it advances have a tendency to side-step the social significance of digital technologies, but for the reason that, in doing so, the strategy ends up replacing the 'agonies of equality and ecological-integrity' with little more than the 'gnostics' of 'new age' wordings, which are centred around storylines about the quality of life. The strategy advocated for adoption by this paper is not grounded in such rhetoric.

The vision of e-topia it builds instead rests on the messages the likes of Graham and Marvin advance, by turning the tables and agreeing that, while words offer the possibility of 'bringing what it all means back together', actually turning things around lies not so much in the words, as it rests with the semantics of the syntax and vocabulary governing the digitally inclusive nature of the regenerative storylines emerging from this discourse and, perhaps even more importantly, the degree to which they overcome the divided antagonisms of the excluded. In this way, the paper suggests that it becomes possible for the multiplied memory and infinite mind of the 'cyborg civics and environments' of their 'tribe-like culture', to not to so much bemoan the 'nomadicity of wireless bi-peds', but actively celebrate the creativity of the virtual communities emerging from the digital-inclusive nature of such regenerative storylines.

In particular, it is added, celebrate the opportunity this in turn creates for virtual communities to use the collective memory, wikis and blogs of their electronically-enhanced services, as a means for such platforms to bridge such social divisions. Bridge them – it is important to note – by drawing upon the political subjectivities of cyborg-civics, their tribe-like culture and nomadicity, as wireless bi-peds with the embedded intelligence smart enough for the citizens of this community to span them. Span them with bridges that are not merely symbolic, but real in the sense which the semantic web of this knowledge-base serves to be the agent of something more than a prop. Something more than a prop and bigger in the sense which the embedding of such intelligence allows the web-based services that support all of this to begin doing the job asked of them. That is the job of building a stage which is large enough for the analytic, synthetic and symbolic components of the transition to be smart in playing out the possibilities there are for urban planning to be both equitable and ecologically integral.

The paper from Walters picks up on what might be referred to as a 'fourth' observation on the trajectory to which Komninos draws attention. His observation also harks back to Mitchell's thesis and suggests that, irrespective of how digital technologies are developed to exploit the electronic opportunities they offer, the physical places of urban spaces will retain their relevance in society because people still care about meeting face-to-face and gravitate to places which offer particular cultural, urban, scenic or climatic spaces, unable to be experienced at the end of a wire and through a computer screen.

The paper from Walters offers what might best be referred to as a 're-urbanist', or 'new urbanist' account of the transition from intelligent to smart cities. Rooted in the 'equity planning of public participation', it argues that the transition is progressive because it is not only intelligent, i.e. founded on the cognitive logic (cybernetics) of systems thinking, but smart enough to present cities with the master plans and design codes capable of regulating the form, massing and placement of the buildings they in turn 'build out'. This, the paper argues, is possible because the embedded intelligence of smart cities rests on the master plans and design codes that are assembled to represent the urban form, spatial infrastructures and buildings seen as capable of sustaining such development.

As the paper goes on to suggest, within the spatial infrastructures and buildings of smart cities, we find that place is something which truly matters. As the paper makes clear: it matters because, while exactly what 'smart' means for cities can be subject to several interpretations, the simplest and most potent definition of smart cities is of a 'place enriched by the assignment of meaning'. For, while technology keeps pushing us apart, in using media to bridge physical distance, we as a culture continue to gather in specific locations meaningful to us. The smartest places, therefore, are those that combine the best of both the physical and virtual worlds, where presence and 'tele-presence' are fused together in a specific location. Here physical locations are pervasively penetrated by digital technologies to provide a collaborative meshing of physical and virtual environments. As an antidote to the 'splintering urbanism' suggested by Graham and Marvin, Walters suggests that in such locations the centrifugal tendencies of digital technologies are balanced by centripetal forces of human interaction which manifest themselves in physical space.

This paper takes it as read that ICTs will continue to evolve in ways that continually challenge our perception of place and as a consequence, space will offer as-yet unforeseen opportunities. As a consequence, it suggests that there will likely be as many negative as positive outcomes from this technological evolution, and that one of the roles of physical, place-based urban planning, development and design is to capitalize on the positives and offset as many of the negatives as possible by means of determined, activist and design-based public policies. As the paper emphasizes, the challenges that surface from such a reading of the transition to smart cities range from counterbalancing the power of global capitalism, to creating generic 'themed' environments which are devoid of place-specific designs, to assisting poor communities in under-serviced parts of cities to participate in grassroots regeneration.

As the paper also makes clear, while debate continues to swirl around the relevance of traditionally construed physical places as settings for human activity in a world both expanded and collapsed by digital media, it is recognized that Mitchell's view of a potentially fruitful and mutually beneficial collaboration between the physical and virtual worlds currently stands in stark contrast to Graham and Marvin's more dystopian vision of a world splintered and fragmented by technological mobilities and networked infrastructures. In particular, it contrasts with that view of the world which suggests that the electronic spaces of urban places threaten to develop 'silent, invisible and pervasive networks with unprecedented potential for exclusion'. The implication of this is clear: if 'place' matters at all, well-planned and designed locations shall become the realm of the more privileged classes and those not fitting some pre-defined intellectual notion of what is smart shall be denied admittance.

In spite of this critique, Walters argues that Mitchell's position is still relevant, particularly if the process of place-making is rooted in participatory democracy, utilizes electronic media to structure and extend democratic debate and, most importantly of all, creates clear implementation strategies regulated by way of, and through, the master planning of form-based design codes.

While the paper suggests that there is no denying the power of Graham and Marvin's alternative view (which states that a 'privatization and liberalization of infrastructural systems' is unravelling the city as a place where people come together for common purposes, implanting instead the conditions of spatial segregation, social polarization and exclusion) the City of Beaufort, SC, stands as a place of resistance to these trends, using electronic media as an agent of social and physical cohesion. While Graham and Marvin quite rightly suggest

that traditional place-making should be treated with scepticism because it can fix exclusionary policies in time and place to the detriment of certain social groups, the inclusionary and electronically enhanced democratic process used by Beaufort in its planning and design activities mitigates such concerns by going out of its way to enhance the public's input into charrette-based blogs and online community discussions.

Referring to the 'triple bottom line' of economic prosperity, environmental stewardship and social justice found in Beaufort's smart growth and sustainability audit, this paper suggests their experience of the transition manages to challenge the belief that such urban planning, development and design exercises merely reproduce the status quo. Whereas some plans do minimize change to suit the interests of upper- and middle-income residents to the detriment of those less well-off, the Beaufort plan specifically encourages, for example, housing diversity and affordability, with an emphasis on workforce housing and 'aging in place'. Indeed, as the paper goes to some length to show, a large segment of work in the case-study charrette deals with many of the substantive issues surrounding the development of housing and the quality of life of people with low and moderate incomes.

Overall, the paper suggests that the Beaufort case study illustrates how the digital town hall can be used to embed place-based master planning and design codes into the town's e-governance. In doing so, this case study is seen as offering a clear example of how Mitchell's thesis on the electronic codification of urban planning and design can give 'character' to a place and, what is more, make this intelligible by embedding the rules and protocols which are smart in encouraging some activities and discouraging others.

This particular charrette, with its detailed preparation, analyses and subsequent code-building methodology, is said to represent state-of-the-art community design practice for neighbourhood renewal in the USA. Its extensive scope, digital presence and attention to small-scale contextual detail are also seen as important in creating 'market-ready' redevelopment projects and providing the benchmarks of progressive planning practice. In particular, the charette can be seen to realize the prospect there is to 'bring this all together' under the reciprocal capacities of a form-based code recalibrated by the site-specific urban design proposals contained in a plan. This, in turn, is seen as something of a step change in what has previously gone under the name of 'progress'.

NOTE

1 http://en.wikipedia.org/wiki/Intelcities.

REFERENCES

Castells, M., 1996, *Rise of the Network Society: The Information Age*, Blackwell, Cambridge.

Curwell, S., Deakin, M., Symes, M., 2005, *Sustainable Urban Development: The Framework, Protocols and Environmental Assessment Methods*, Routledge, London.

Deakin, M., 2007, 'From city of bits to e-topia: taking the thesis on digitally-inclusive regeneration full circle', *Journal of Urban Technology* 14(3), 131–143.

Deakin, M., 2010, 'SCRAN's development of a trans-national comparator for the standardisation of e-government services', in C. Reddick (ed), *Comparative eGovernment: An Examination of E-Government Across Countries*, Springer, Berlin, 424–438.

Deakin, M., 2011, 'From the city of bits to e-topia: space, citizenship and community as global strategy in the governance of the digitally-inclusive regeneration strategy', in

D. PiaggesiK. Sund, W. Castelnovo (eds), *Global Strategy and Practice of e-Governance: Examples from Around the World*, IGI Publisher, Hershey, 124–141.

Deakin, M., Allwinkle, S., 2007, 'Urban regeneration and sustainable communities: the role networks, innovation and creativity in building successful partnerships', *Journal of Urban Technology* 14(1), 77–91.

Graham, S., Marvin, S., 1996, *Telecommunications and the City*, Routledge, London.

Graham, S., Marvin, S., 2001, *Splintering Urbanism*, Routledge, London.

Hollands, R., 2008, 'Will the real smart city stand up?' *City* 12(3), 302–320.

Komninos, N., 2002, *Intelligent Cities: Innovation, Knowledge Systems and Digital Spaces*, Spon Press, London.

Komninos, N., 2008, *Intelligent Cities and Globalisation of Innovation Networks*, Taylor & Francis, London.

Mitchell, W., 1995, *City of Bits: Space, Place, and the Infobahn*, MIT Press, Cambridge, MA.

Mitchell, W., 1999, *e-Topia: Urban Life, Jim But Not As You Know It*, MIT Press, Cambridge, MA.

Mitchell, W., 2001, 'Equitable access to an on-line world', in D. Schon, B. Sanyal, W. Mitchell (eds), *High Technology and Low-Income Communities*, MIT Press, Cambridge, MA, 151–162.

Mitchell, W., 2003, *Me + +: the Cyborg-Self and the Networked City*, MIT Press, Cambridge, MA.

OECD – EUROSTAT, 2005, *Oslo Manual*, Statistical Office of the European Communities, Paris.

Paskaleva, K., 2009, 'Enabling the smart city: the progress of e-city governance in Europe', *International Journal of Innovation and Regional Development* 1(4), 405–422.

From intelligent to smart cities

Mark Deakin[1] and Husam Al Waer[2]

[1]Edinburgh Napier University, Edinburgh, UK
[2]University of Dundee, Dundee, UK

Taking Hollands' previous statement on the transition from intelligent to smart cities as its point of departure ('Will the real smart city stand up?' *City* 12(3), 302–320), this article reflects upon the anxieties currently surrounding such developments. In particular, it considers the suggestion that such developments have more to do with cities meeting the corporate needs of marketing campaigns than the social intelligence required for them to be smart. Focusing on the social intelligence of such developments, this article captures the information-rich and highly communicative qualities of the transition. In particular, it examines the methodological issues that smart communities pose cities and the critically insightful role which the networks of innovation and creative partnerships set up to embed such intelligence play in the learning, knowledge transfer and capacity-building exercises servicing this community-led transition to smart cities. This, the article suggests, is what existing representations of smart cities miss. This article offers a critically insightful account of the transition.

INTRODUCTION

Smart city forerunners, such as San Diego, San Francisco, Ottawa, Brisbane, Amsterdam, Kyoto and Bangalore, are all now setting a trend for others to follow. Other cities now keen to follow in their wake and become smart include Southampton, Manchester, Newcastle, Edinburgh, Edmonton, Vancouver and Montreal.

Taking Hollands' (2008) article on the transition from intelligent to smart cities as its point of departure, this article reflects upon the anxieties currently surrounding such developments. In particular, it considers the suggestion that such developments have more to do with cities meeting the corporate needs of marketing campaigns than the social intelligence required for them to be smart. Working on the assumption that any attempt to overcome such anxieties means cities shifting attention away from the needs of the market and towards the intelligence required for them to be smart, the article begins to set out a less presumptuous and more critically aware understanding of the transition from intelligent to smart cities.

WILL THE REAL SMART CITY STAND UP?

In a recent article, Hollands (2008) asks the question: 'will the real smart city stand up?' For, according to Hollands (2008), cities all too often claim to be smart, but do so without defining what this means, or offering any evidence to support such proclamations. The all-too-often 'self-congratulatory' tone cities strike when making such claims does not seem to sit well with Hollands (2008). While images of the digital city, intelligent city, high-tech district and neighbourhoods of smart communities abound, they all fail to convey what it means to be smart and why it is important for cities to be defined in such terms.

In Hollands' (2008) opinion, the validity of any claim to be smart has to be based on something more than their use of information and communication technologies (ICTs). Hollands (2008) asks this question because cities all over the world are beginning to do just this and use such technologies as a means of branding themselves smart. Such smart city forerunners like San Diego, San Francisco, Ottawa, Brisbane, Amsterdam, Kyoto and Bangalore, are all now setting a trend for others to follow. The other cities keen to follow in their wake and become smart are: Southampton, Manchester, Newcastle, Edinburgh, Edmonton, Vancouver and Montreal. It appears that the rush to become a smart city has begun to gather apace and, as a consequence, pressure is now growing for cities to become even smarter.

IBM's recent high-profile campaign on smart cities also goes someway to acknowledge this pressure for cities to become smarter. As they state:

> Technological advances [now] allow cities to be "instrumented," facilitating the collection of more data points than ever before, which enables cities to measure and influence more aspects of their operations. Cities are increasingly "interconnected," allowing the free flow of information from one discrete system to another, which increases the efficiency of the overall infrastructure.... To [meet] these challenges and provide sustainable prosperity for citizens and businesses, cities must become "smarter" and use new technologies to transform their systems to optimize the use of finite resources.[1]

Hollands' (2008) anxiety about the 'self-congratulatory' nature of the claims cities make to be smart tends to hark back to the image-building and city marketing campaigns of the 1990s and the competition this sparked between cities. Hollands' (2008) fear of using such an ill-defined notion to spearhead yet another marketing campaign lies in the in-built tendency that such strategies have to be almost exclusively entrepreneurial in outlook and to undermine the more collaborative and consensus-building aspirations of the networking paradigm which has developed to replace them.

Hollands (2008) asks us to be aware that, if left to be entrepreneurial, there is a strong chance that smart cities will develop in a way which is too neo-conservative and insufficiently progressive to offer the type of liberating experience everyone expects of them. For Hollands (2008) the way to avoid the disappointment of any neo-conservative route to smart cities lies in following the clarion cry of those advocating a more neo-liberal pathway. This is because, for him, such a pathway is seen to be rooted in a critically aware and more realistic understanding of smart cities.

FROM THE INTELLIGENT TO SMART CITY

In the interests of developing just such a critically aware and realistic understanding, Hollands (2008) draws particular attention to the work of Komninos (2002, 2008) on the intelligent city. For, according to this account of what it means to be an intelligent city, there are four main components to such developments, these being:

- the application of a wide range of electronic and digital technologies to communities and cities,
- the use of information technologies to transform life and work within a region,
- the embedding of such ICTs in the city,
- the territorialization of such practices in a way that bring ICTs and people together, so as to enhance the innovation, learning, knowledge and problem solving which they offer.

This much-needed definition of what it means to be an intelligent city is in turn used by Hollands

(2008) to clear the way for a vision of cities that are smart because they are:

> ... territories with a high capacity for learning and innovation, which is built-in to the creativity of their population, their institutions of knowledge production and their digital infrastructure for communication.

For Hollands (2008, p.306) the key elements of this definition relate to the use of networked infrastructures as a means to enable social, environmental, economic and cultural development. While this involves the use of a wide range of infrastructures, including transport, business services, housing and a range of public and independent services (including leisure and lifestyle services), it is the ICTs of these developments that are of critical importance because they are seen to 'undergird' (Hollands, 2008) all of these networks and single them out as the common denominator lying at core of the smart city.

Those ICTs seen as 'undergirding' all of this and lying at the core of the networks include: mobile and land line phones, satellite TVs, computer networks, electronic commerce and internet services. They are seen to be of critical importance because Hollands (2008) considers the intelligence such infrastructures embed as the main driving force behind the development of smart cities and capable of sustaining social, environmental and cultural progress.

TOWARDS SMART CITIES

As Hollands (2008, p.315) goes on to state: smart cities, by definition, appear to be 'wired cities', although this cannot be the sole defining criterion because:

> progressive(ly) smart cities must seriously start with people and the human capital side of the equation, rather than blindly believing that IT itself can automatically transform and improve cities.

For Hollands (2008, p.316) the critical factor in any successful community, enterprise or venture is its people and how they interact. This is because, for Hollands (2008), the most important thing about information technology is not the capacity which it has to create smart cities, but the ability that such communications have to be part of a social, economic and cultural development. That is to say, serve as communications which are smart in the way the deployment of their information technologies allows cities to empower and educate people, allowing them to become members of society capable of engaging in a debate about the environment to which they relate. This, it is stressed, in turn, is only made possible when the community of people undergoing such a process of socialization are able to:

> create a real shift in the balance of power between the use of information technology by business, government, communities and ordinary people who live in cities, as well as seek to balance economic growth with sustainability. ... In a word, the 'real' smart city might use IT to enhance democratic debates about the kind of city it wants to be and what kind of city people want to live in.

To achieve this, Hollands (2008, p.316) suggests that those cities that really want to be smart will have to:

> take much greater risks with technology, devolve power, tackle inequalities and redefine what they mean by smart itself, if they want to retain such a lofty title.

SOME IMMEDIATE REFLECTIONS

While Hollands' (2008) image of what it means to be smart tends to start with the nightmare scenario of a city dominated by the entrepreneurial values of the elite few, it is clear this vision of a somewhat unintelligent, neo-conservative and less than liberal representation is soon swept aside by a more progressive alternative. An alternative, which, in this instance, uses information technology, not to shore up the entrepreneurial values of the city, but to underpin them in a way which is smart. That is to say, smart in the sense that information technologies and not entrepreneurial values are used as the means by which cities 'undergird' their social, communal and environmental qualities.

As a 'best-case' scenario, this works well to allay any fears that may linger about the purpose of smart cities and the ways in which they should be put to work. As with all such visions, however, there are some inconsistencies and omissions in the narrative and storylines this develops as a means to usher in the reworked version of what is being represented, i.e. the smart city. These relate to both the legacy of smart cities and the more contemporary issues underlying their development.

In particular, they relate to Hollands' representation of the 'smart city' legacy, that is perhaps just a little too 'fast and furious', in the sense that the retrospective offered relies less on the notion of 'informational cities' advanced by the likes of Castells (1996), or Graham and Marvin (1996, 2001) and more on Mitchell's (1995, 1999, 2001, 2003) accounts of what it means for the technologies of such infrastructures 'to work smarter not harder'! While Castells (1996) and Graham and Marvin (1996, 2001) all draw attention to the information technologies of the so-called critical infrastructures (water and drainage, energy and the like), it is Mitchell (1995, 1999, 2001, 2003), who first deployed them in the Smart City laboratory at MIT and has sketched out how they make it possible for communities to network the embedded intelligence of smart cities.

THE SMART CARD LEGACY

This can be illustrated by reference to the influence of the Smart City laboratory on what

Hollands (2008) himself defines as the first smart city. Southampton was the first city that attempted to develop a portal capable of supporting smart card applications. This initiative, promoted under the triple-helix model of University, Industry (of the tele-communications sector) and Government, was the first to develop a smart card software customizing access to a variety of services distributed across the public and independent sectors. It was also the first software development reported as capable of supporting the transactional-based logic of multi-application management architectures and as enterprises allowing services to be added to and removed as part of the card's dynamic user environment.

The administration of the card scheme involves the processing of personal data: compliance with UK and EU data protection legislation is critical and both the University and Industrial sector in question are keenly aware of the privacy issues arising from any association with such Government-sponsored card schemes. To comply with this legislation each smart card has a unique identifier, which can be used by all service applications to identify the user, and when transaction information is sent to the data warehouse, this unique identifier is 'one-way' encrypted. This means that the unique identifier is scrambled so that transaction information cannot be traced back to any user whose personal data are held within the warehouse. However, even though the information held in the data warehouse is stored anonymously, it is still considered to be 'personal data', due to the fact it is possible to match it with information in other databases.

If service providers wish to share personal data for which they are the controller, this must be done for a distinct purpose, underpinned by some formal data sharing protocol. However, where multiple applications are provided by the same data controller, the data collected from these applications can be used in the course of any legitimate interest. This may include cross matching and trend analysis, where this directly relates to a notified purpose.

It is the ability this portal has to deal with multiple transactions simultaneously and as a 'bundle of services' in a real-time environment, which has attracted so much attention from those cities seeking to be smart in supporting the development of such e-Government (e-Gov) services. This has meant cities shifting attention away from the e-commerce challenges of the enterprise architecture and transaction-based business logic supporting such e-Gov service developments and towards the embedded intelligence of what Halpern (2005) sees as being something really smart.

THE INFORMATIONAL BASIS OF SUCH COMMUNICATIONS

The point of this digression into smart cards is simple. It lies in the realization that it is the legacy of Castells' (1996) and Graham and Marvin's (1996, 2001) work undertaken on the informational basis of the communications embedded in such intelligence, rather than the work carried out by Mitchell (1995, 1999, 2001, 2003), which leads us away from the purely technical issues surrounding the business logic of such e-Gov service developments. That is, away from the technical issues which surround the transaction-based business logic of such developments and towards a more critically insightful examination of the information-rich and highly communicative qualities of the technologies (vis-à-vis ICTs) supporting them. In other words, away from the technical aspects of such developments and towards an examination of the social capital which is not only critical in underpinning the development's informational and communicative qualities, but also insightful in revealing the wider environmental and cultural role they play in supporting the transition to smart cities.

CAPTURING THE INFORMATION-RICH AND HIGHLY COMMUNICATIVE QUALITIES OF SUCH SERVICE DEVELOPMENTS

What follows captures the information-rich and highly communicative qualities of these technical, social, wider environmental and cultural developments, the particular methodological issues they pose and the critically insightful role which the networks of innovation and creative partnerships set up to embed such intelligence play in the learning, knowledge transfer and capacity-building exercises that service this transition to smart cities. This is what the article suggests Hollands' (2008) account of smart cities misses and it goes some way to explain why he asks 'the real smart city to stand up!' For, in cutting across the legacy of the transition from the informational to the intelligent and now smart city, Hollands' (2008) account of the transition is not as well grounded in the informational and communicative qualities of the embedded intelligence they are built on.

This, the article suggests, is a critical insight of some note, for only in giving such a well-grounded account of the embedded intelligence drawn attention to is it possible to do what Hollands (2008) asks of the transition: that is, 'undergird' the social capital which is not only critical in underpinning the informational and communicative qualities of the embedded intelligence smart cities stand on, but pivotal in gaining a fuller insight into their significance. In particular, pivotal in gaining a fuller insight into the wider environmental and cultural significance their networks of innovation and creative partnerships take on in embedding the intelligence of such an informatics-based and community-led transition to smart cities.

The article goes on to suggest that this insight is equally significant because it takes Hollands' (2008) thinking full-circle by offering an alternative to the 'top-down' entrepreneurial-based business logic which is called for. This alternative is realized by turning the top-down entrepreneurial-based business logic on its head and grounding the information-rich and highly communicative qualities of such developments in the community-led logic that is emerging to support the transition. That logic which in real time is aligned with, not against, the cybernetics of the social capital underlying the emergence of smart communities, and what their founding networks of innovation and creative partnerships embed as the intelligence of smart cities. Those developments in the cybernetics of social capital that are now in the process of being institutionalized in the learning, knowledge transfer and capacity-building exercises which are intelligent in embedding the informatics of this community-led transition to smart cities.

As always, there is another reason for taking an alternate route. The article not only offers an alternative to the entrepreneurial-based business logic embedded in the corporate branding of such developments, but a social and environmental counterpoint to the 'high level' cultural account of smart cities otherwise offered by Cohendet and Simon (2008) in their study of Montreal. Rather than relying on any notion of the 'creative class' offered by Florida (2002, 2004), the account we offer in this article is rooted in an institutional reading of the social capital underpinning the 'environments' such notions about the 'rise of a creative class' attempt to cultivate.

This is because, for us, it is social capital that underpins such environments and which gets 'bottomed-out' in our representation of the transition by way of Castells (1996) and Graham and Marvin (1996, 2001), rather than through Mitchell's (1995, 1999, 2001, 2003) investigations into the embedded intelligence of smart cities. Social capital that not only underpins such environments, but which is also brought to the fore in this article's account of the transition. In particular, in that account which surfaces by way of its case-based analysis of the community-led movement in Edinburgh and through an examination of the environments which are being 'cultivated' to support this particular city's transition.

In paving the way for this representation of the transition, the rest of the article shall account for what is termed the social capital of smart communities and will consider the methodological twist this particular take on the transition offers. In particular, it will examine

what this take on the transition offers to undergird the embedded intelligence of smart cities. It will reflect on the embedded intelligence, networks of innovation and creative partnerships that do much to support the environments which Edinburgh cultivates, for the reason that they go some way to capture what is smart about the city's transition.

This is what is unique about this article on the transition and captures what it is that 'stands up' about the transition rather than 'breaks down' into little more than the business logic of self-congratulatory claims.

THE SOCIAL CAPITAL OF SMART COMMUNITIES

Halpern (2005, p.508) speaks of social capital being composed of 'a network; a cluster of norms, rules, values and expectations; and sanctions'. Here communities are understood to form networks, to co-operate with one another in accordance with the norms, rules and expectations of their constituents and to have the power to sanction actions taken by fellow members who operate outside the said norms, rules, values and expectations. These in turn are also seen to provide the linkages between members of the community who use these norms, rules and values to bridge divisions that exist in civic society.

Halpern (2005, pp.509–510) understands ICTs to be forms of social capital and lists several pre-requisites for the development of networked communities. These pre-requisites are examined in terms of the potential which networked communities, virtual organizations and managed learning environments have to develop the ecological integrity and equity of regeneration as part of the ongoing process of democratic renewal that is needed for socially inclusive decision making. As he states:

While the vast majority of community ICT experiments have to date not met the conditions above [the ecological integrity, equity, democratic renewal, needs and requirements]. ICT networks may have great potential to boost local social capital, provided they are geographically "intelligent," that is, are smart enough to connect you directly to your neighbours; are built around natural communities; and facilitate the collection of collective knowledge. They have the potential to connect the work-poor and work-rich.

THE METHODOLOGICAL TWIST

The methodological twist in Halpern's (2005) discussions on 'geographically intelligent settlements' lies in the fact that this examination of networks, virtual organizations and managed learning environments precedes the planning, development and design of villages and neighbourhoods. Those networks, virtual organizations and managed learning environments which are in turn seen as providing the info-structures for communities to collaborate and build consensus on the development of high-tech and digitally enabled platforms. High-tech and digitally enabled platforms that offer the informational basis for the planning, development and design of villages and neighbourhoods. That type of informatics-based planning, development and design which goes a long way to strengthen the norms, rules and values of the said settlements by providing the citizens of these communities with a platform to bridge the gap between the 'work-poor and work-rich'. In particular, bridge that gap which has opened up as a digital divide between the informational basis of the so-called 'work-rich' and 'work-poor' and do this by building a platform capable of tying them together as communities strong enough to carry the environmental weight and economic expectation (vis-à-vis ecological integrity and equity) of their ongoing regeneration.

NETWORKS, INNOVATION AND CREATIVE PARTNERSHIPS

So where are these ICT-enabled networks that boost the norms, rules and values of local social capital? Boost them because they are geographically 'intelligent', that is, sufficiently innovative to connect 'villagers' directly to 'neighbours' by virtue of being based on creative partnerships which are built around 'natural' communities? Around natural communities that facilitate the creation of collective knowledge which they can draw upon in order to meet the expectations of their on-going regeneration? Contrary to popular belief, such urban regeneration programmes are not limited to the UK, but can be found throughout Europe. For example they can be found in Edinburgh, Helsinki, Glasgow and Dublin (Deakin et al., 2005; Deakin and Allwinkle, 2006).

The following offers a very brief account of the networks, innovation and creative partnerships underlying the villages and neighbourhoods of the geographically intelligent and smart community regeneration programmes underway in Edinburgh as part of the city's social inclusion partnerships (SIPs). This article shall examine the city's smart regeneration programmes for the Wester Hailes and Craigmillar communities (Deakin and Allwinkle, 2007). An account of the urban regeneration partnerships governing the planning, development and design of Wester Hailes and Craigmillar can be found in Hastings (1996), Carley (1995), Carley and Kirk (1998) and Carley et al. (2000). The development of these networks and innovations is also reported on by Slack (2000), Malina (2001, 2002) Malina and MacIntosh (2004) and McWilliams et al. (2004). Malina and Ball (2005) have also reported on the development of social capital emerging from these innovations and have addressed the question of whether the villages and neighbourhoods emerging are not just geographically 'intelligent', but 'smart-er' in the sense their communities connect 'villagers' to their 'neighbours'.

The following shall cut across these reports and draw attention to the creative partnership(s) emerging from the urban planning, development and design of the villages and neighbourhoods making up the communities in question. Similar developments underway in Helsinki are reported on by Sotarauta (2001), Kostiainen and Sotarauta (2003) and Sotarauta and Srinivas (2006). Dabinett (2005) also reports on the situation emerging in Glasgow and Dublin.

This article also goes some considerable way in turning what Hollands (2008) suggests is the 'should' of smart cities around into an examination of what they actually do. In short, it demonstrates that, by 'taking risks with technologies, devolving power and tackling inequalities', it is possible to turn things around and hold cities up as a clear demonstration of 'what it means to be smart'. In other words, it provides the material to match the means with the ends.

MYEDINBURGH.ORG

As an ICT-enabled network, myEdinburgh.org is innovative because it gets beyond the user-centred environment of the smart card legacy by providing an information portal and community grid for learning (CGfL). This particular information portal provides citizens with the user-friendly tools for communities to access learning opportunities. Within this environment, the CGfL provides the infrastructure needed for citizens to learn about the planning, development and design of their cities and engage in local decisions made about the promotion of urban villages and neighbourhoods as sustainable communities under the city's urban regeneration strategy.

The Edinburgh Learning Partnership, composed of representatives from local government agencies, the education sector, voluntary groups and private-sector businesses, provides the creative basis for the networking and innovation the said portal and grid offers access to. As a city-wide venture, the collaboration seeks to encourage and facilitate initiatives that are creative in widening access to and increasing participation in learning activities, particularly those which target the disadvantaged. The key aims of the partnership can be summarized as follows:

- to provide citizens with ICT 'taster' sessions in local, accessible venues; specifically targeting citizens identified as 'digitally excluded' (e.g. citizens living in Edinburgh's SIPs);
- to support community and voluntary organizations in the procurement, use, and development of ICTs, including training staff to access and maintain the information portal;
- to develop a CGfL;
- to use the said grid for learning to build capacity and engage citizens in local decision making;
- to transfer the knowledge required to participate in the planning, development, design and layout of villages and neighbourhoods and democratic renewal needed for this process of modernization to govern their development of self-sustaining communities (Figure 1).

E-LEARNING, KNOWLEDGE TRANSFER, AND CAPACITY BUILDING

The resulting e-learning platform makes it possible for the online service applications being demonstrated to be integrated with the knowledge transfer and capacity-building technologies needed to meet the interoperability requirements of such developments.

This allows the citizens, communities and organizations in question to collaborate and build consensus on the competencies, skills needed and training required for the development of these online services to support urban regeneration programmes. Together, these networks of innovation and creativity underpin the partnerships responsible for embedding the intelligence of those technologies, skills and training exercises, making it possible for citizens to engage in this process and show how active participation in the said venture is smart. That is to say, how participation is not only intelligent because it draws upon such services, but smart for the reason that it develops the social capital which sets the normative standards and rule-based logic of the very civic values governing the ecological integrity and equity of the environments. The environments that – in this

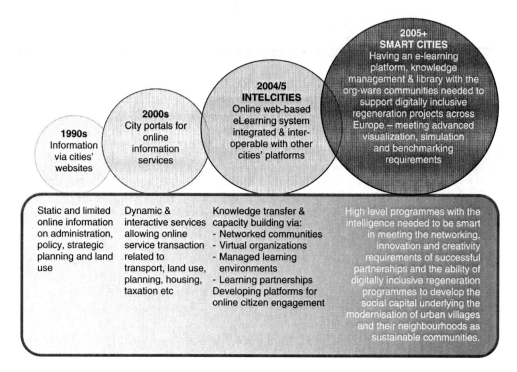

FIGURE 1 The development of digitally inclusive regeneration programmes
Source: Deakin and Allwinkle (2007).

instance – are responsible for cultivating the deeply rooted process of democratic renewal which their very participation in this venture is key in unlocking.

This is made possible because:

- the ICT-enabled networks are innovative in developing an e-learning platform based on open-source technologies that are interoperable across online services;
- satisfying the need for a formal learning community, this high-tech, digitally enabled network allows for the planning, development and design of the online services needed for regeneration programmes to support SIPs;
- these partnerships, in turn, allow the ecological integrity, equity, democratic norms, rules and values of the applications being demonstrated to be integrated with the e-learning, knowledge transfer and capacity-building technologies supporting the regeneration programmes.

- this allows citizens and communities to collaborate and build consensus on the competencies, skills, and training needed for the development of those online services required to support the quintessentially civic values of this regeneration programme;
- together the said networks, innovations and partnerships create the trust needed to engage citizens and show how the active participation of communities in digitally inclusive decision making is both intelligent in developing the social capital norms, rules and civic values – of the ecological integrity and equity underlying the modernization and smart enough to support it;
- here the ecological integrity and equity of the democratic renewal take the form of consultations and deliberations in government and citizen-led decision making that engage

citizens as members of a community participating in this modernization;

- the resulting platform supports the distribution, storage, retrieval of learning material, skill packages and training materials needed for such engagement and participation to bridge the digital divides that currently exist, to build the capacity which exists for inclusive decision making, and to transfer the knowledge required for citizens to bond with one another as members of a community. The ecological integrity of this socially cohesive process takes the form of decisions over the development's ecological footprint, bio-diversity and environmental loading.

The democratic renewal does this by promoting the shift from government to citizen-led decision making within the community. This involves the use of advisory groups, discussion boards, opinion polls, focus groups, petitions, citizen juries, ballots and online voting. These are all part of the visioning and scenario-building exercises for gaining consensus on the norms of energy consumption, waste and emissions, as a set of rules underlying the social equity and environmental justice of the democratic renewal governing this process of modernization.

As the standards of knowledge transfer and capacity building are drawn from a review of leading city portals across Europe and the benchmarking of their respective CGfLs against stakeholder requirements, the intelligence embedded in these applications should be smart enough and the physiology of the built environment it (re) regenerates sufficiently strong for the urban planning, development and design of the villages and neighbourhoods in question not to be overloaded, but able to carry the weight of their transformation into self-sustaining communities.

All this is in contrast to how villages and neighbourhoods are traditionally represented as self-sustaining communities and offers an illustration of how the intelligence being embedded in this particular smart city can stand up and be counted for the progress it is making.

CONCLUSIONS

Taking Hollands' (2008) statement about the 'unspoken assumption' as the point of departure, this article has reflected upon the anxieties currently surrounding the transition from intelligent to smart cities. In particular, it has considered the suggestion that such developments have more to do with cities meeting the corporate branding needs of marketing campaigns than the social intelligence required for them to be smart.

Working on the assumption that any attempt to overcome such anxieties means cities shifting attention away from the needs of the market and towards the intelligence required for them to be smart, the article begins to set out a less presumptuous and more critically aware understanding of the transition from intelligent to smart cities.

In particular, an understanding based on the legacy of Castells' (1996) and Graham and Marvin's (1996, 2001) research carried out on the informational basis of the communications embedded in such intelligence, rather than that carried out by Mitchell (1995, 1999, 2001, 2003) leads us away from the purely technical issues surrounding the business logic of the e-Gov service developments associated with the transition to smart cities. That is, away from the technical issues which surround the business logic of such developments and towards a more critically insightful appreciation of the information-rich and highly communicative qualities of the technologies supporting them. Away, in that sense, from the technical aspects of such developments and towards an examination of the social capital which is not only critical in underpinning their informational and communicative qualities, but also insightful in revealing the wider environmental and cultural role they play in supporting the transition to smart cities.

Armed with this critical insight, the article has sought to capture the highly communicative qualities of such service developments, the particular methodological issues that smart communities pose cities and the critically insightful role which the networks of innovation and creative partnerships set up to embed such intelligence play in the learning, knowledge transfer and capacity-building exercises servicing this community-led transition to smart cities.

This is what Hollands' (2008) account of smart cities misses and it goes some way to explain why he asks 'the real smart city to stand up'. For, in cutting across the social capital and environmental capacities of the transition from intelligent to smart cities, the representation that surfaces is insufficiently grounded in the informational and communicative qualities of the embedded intelligence which not only underpins such developments, but also offers the means to do what Hollands (2008) asks of them. That is 'undergird' the social capital which is not only critical in underpinning their informational and communicative qualities, but also insightful in revealing the wider environmental and cultural role their networks of innovation and creative partnerships play in supporting the development of a community-led transition to smart cities.

We also suggest this insight is equally significant because it takes Hollands' (2008) thinking full-circle and in doing so offers an alternative to the 'top-down' entrepreneurial-based business logic called loud and hard for. This is achieved by grounding the developments under review in what we refer to as the community-led logic of the transition.

By focusing on the social capital of collaborative platforms and consensus building, it has also become possible to recognize the critical role networks, innovation and creative partnerships play in representing places that are not only sites of ecological integrity, social equity, environmental justice and democratic renewal, but locations where socially inclusive decision making can institutionalize the civic values which are required for the regeneration of urban villages and neighbourhood as self-sustaining communities.

Having reported on an ICT-enabled network that provides just such an information portal and CGfL, the article has reviewed the innovative features of partnerships which are creative in organizing the development of the necessary technologies, skills and training exercises. The partnerships found to be successful are those which make it possible for regeneration programmes to engage citizens and demonstrate how the embedded intelligence of community participation is smart. The evidence generated from the Edinburgh case-study is valuable because it reveals that successful partnerships not only develop the norms, rules and civic values of any regeneration, but that they also express the programme's ecological integrity, social equity and environmental justice as part of an underlying venture in democratic renewal.

The main findings of this case study can be summarized as follows:

- Questions about the critical role of networking, innovation and the creativity of partnerships have previously remained unanswered because many believe they are resources that can easily be assembled and which can be left to develop as virtuous circles of mutually reinforcing actions.
- This underestimates the extent of the embedded intelligence, networks, innovation and creativity needed to build partnerships and be successful in meeting their capacity-building and knowledge-transfer requirements.
- Many such partnerships tend to represent little more than short-term measures at self-help and exercises in community learning on matters related to 'how best to pull yourself up by your own bootstraps'. That so-called self-help aesthetic stands in opposition to a 'collective' knowledge of the social, environmental, cultural and civic values underpinning this process of democratic renewal and to those supporting such a transition to smart cities.

The article has also found that it is the e-learning platform emerging from these developments which makes it possible for the online service applications being demonstrated to integrate with the knowledge transfer and capacity building needed to meet the interoperability requirements of such developments. This platform allows the citizens, communities and organizations in question to collaborate and build consensus on the competencies, skills and training needed for the development of the online services required to support urban regeneration programmes. Together, the networks of innovation and creative partnerships responsible for organizing the development of these technologies, their requisite skills and training exercises make it possible to engage citizens and show how their active participation is valuable.

NOTE

1 IBM's website on Smart Cities: www-935.ibm.com/services/us/gbs/bus/html/smarter-cities.html.

REFERENCES

Carley, M., 1995, 'The bigger-picture: organizing for sustainable urban regeneration', *Town and Country Planning* **64**(9), 236–239.

Carley, M., Kirk, K., 1998, *Sustainable by 2020? A Strategic Approach to Urban Regeneration for Britain's Cities*, Policy Press, Bristol.

Carley, M., Chapman, M., Hastings, A., Kirk, K., Young, R., 2000, *Urban Regeneration Through Partnership: A Study in Nine Urban Regions in England, Scotland and Wales*, Policy Press, Bristol.

Castells, M., 1996, *Rise of the Network Society: The Information Age*, Blackwell, Cambridge.

Cohendet, P., Simon, L., 2008, 'Knowledge-intensive firms, communities and creative cities', in A. Amin, J. Roberts (eds), *Community, Economic Creativity and Organisation*, Oxford University Press, Oxon.

Dabinett, G., 2005, 'Competing in the information age: urban regeneration and economic development practices', *Journal of Urban Technology* **12**(3), 19–38.

Deakin, M., Allwinkle, S., 2006, 'The IntelCities community of practice: the e-learning platform, knowledge management systems and digital library for semantically-interoperable

e-governance services', *International Journal of Knowledge, Culture and Change in Organizations* **6**(2), 155–162.

Deakin, M., Allwinkle, S., 2007, 'Urban regeneration and sustainable communities: the role networks, innovation and creativity in building successful partnerships', *Journal of Urban Technology* **14**(1), 77–91.

Deakin, M., Allwinkle, S., Campbell, F., Van Isacker, K., 2005, 'The IntelCities e-learning platform, knowledge management system and digital library', in M. Cunningham, P. Cunningham (eds), *Innovation and the Knowledge Economy: Issues, Applications, Case Studies*, IOS Press, Amsterdam.

Florida, R., 2002, *The Rise of the Creative Class: and How it's Transforming Work, Leisure, Community and Everyday Life*, Basic Books, New York.

Florida, R., 2004, *Cities and the Creative Class*, Routledge, London.

Graham, S., Marvin, S., 1996, *Telecommunications and the City*, Routledge, London.

Graham, S., Marvin, S., 2001, *Splintering Urbanism*, Routledge, London.

Halpern, D., 2005, *Social Capital*, Policy Press, Bristol. Quotations from pages 510 and 308–309.

Hastings, A., 1996, 'Unravelling the process of partnership in urban regeneration policy', *Urban Studies* **33**(2), 253–268.

Hollands, R., 2008, 'Will the real smart city stand up?' *City* **12**(3), 302–320.

Komninos, N., 2002, *Intelligent Cities: Innovation, Knowledge Systems and Digital Spaces*, Spon Press, London.

Komninos, N., 2008, *Intelligent Cities and the Globalisation of Innovation Networks*, Taylor and Francis, London.

Kostiainen, J., Sotarauta, M., 2003, 'Great leap or long march to knowledge economy: institutions, actors, and resources in the development of tampere, Finland', *European Planning Studies* **10**(5), 415–438.

Malina, M., 2001, 'Electronic community networks', *Journal of Community Work and Development* **1**(2), 67–83.

Malina, A., 2002, 'Community networks and perception of civic value', *Communications* **27**, 211–234.

Malina, A., Ball, I., 2005, 'ICTs and community: some suggestions for further research in Scotland', *Journal of Community Infomatics* **1**(3), 66–83.

Malina, A., MacIntosh, A., 2004, 'Bridging the digital divide: the development in Scotland', in M. Malkia, A. Anttioiko, R. Savolainem (eds), *eTransformation in Governance*, Idea Group Publishing, Hershey.

McWilliams, M., Johnstone, C., Mooney, G., 2004, 'Urban policy in the New Scotland: the role of social inclusion partnerships', *Space and Polity* **8**(3), 309–319.

Mitchell, W., 1995, *City of Bits: Space, Place, and the Infobahn*, MIT Press, Cambridge, MA.

Mitchell, W., 1999, *e-Topia: Urban Life, Jim but Not as You Know It*, MIT Press, Cambridge.

Mitchell, W., 2001, 'Equitable access to an on-line world', in D. Schon, B. Sanyal, W. Mitchell (eds), *High Technology and Low-Income Communities*, MIT Press, Cambridge, MA.

Mitchell, W., 2003, *Me ++: the Cyborg-self and the Networked City*, MIT Press, Cambridge, MA.

Slack, S., 2000, 'The dialectics of place and space: on community in the information age new media and society', *New Media and Society* **2**(3), 313–334.

Sotarauta, M., 2001, 'Network management and information systems in promotion of urban economic development: some reflections from CityWeb of tampere', *European Planning Studies* **6**, 693–706.

Sotarauta, M., Srinivas, S., 2006, 'Co-evolutionary policy processes: understanding innovative economies and future resilience', *Futures* **38**(3), 312–336.

The smart city: A nexus for open innovation?

Krassimira Antonova Paskaleva[1,2]

[1]Manchester Business School, Manchester University, 8.30 Harold Hankins Building, Manchester, M15 6PB, UK
[2]Institute for Technology Assessment and Systems Analysis, Karlsruhe Institute of Technology, P.O.B. 3640, 76021 Karlsruhe, Germany

This article critically reviews current European trends on smart cities in the context of open innovation. It draws from analyses of key European Union (EU) programmes, four international projects and related activities. These initiatives are framed by the EU's strategic policies on Competitiveness and Innovation, Smart Cities, the Future Internet and Living Labs with the aims to foster smarter, sustainable and inclusive cities. The article probes similarities and differences in the programmes and projects examined and their challenges towards EU strategies, including the i2020 agenda. The analysis shows that a new approach to open innovation is emerging, which links technologies with people, urban territory and other cities and that this approach is likely to be increasingly influential over the next period of time. It is suggested that this approach of using open innovation for sharing visions, knowledge, skills, experience and strategies for designing the delivery of services, goods and policies in cities is effective, efficient and sustainable. However, consistent frameworks, principles and strategic agendas are necessary to optimally bind these elements together.

INTRODUCTION

Amid profound economic, social and technological changes caused by globalization and integration processes, cities in Europe and around the world are faced by the challenge of reconciling competitiveness with long-term sustainable development. In the era of the digital economy, the performance of cities is influenced not only by their physical infrastructure, but more and more so by their knowledge and social capacity ('intellectual and social capital'). This later form of capital has been newly considered most critical for

achieving sustainable and competitive cities. Against that background, the construct of the 'smart city' has emerged as a strategic course of the past ten years emphasizing the increasing importance of information and communication technologies (ICTs) for encompassing modern urban development factors in a common framework and for profiling cities' competitiveness based on their social and environmental capital (Caragliu et al., 2009). The significance of these two factors in fact is known to distinguish 'Smart

Cities' from their more technology-burdened peers known as 'digital' or 'intelligent' cities.

Over the course of the last several years and in context of building the digital economy, the 'smart cities' agenda has gained a real momentum in the countries from the European Union (EU) (Komninos, 2002; Paskaleva, 2009). Other international organizations, such as the Organisation for Economic Co-operation and Development (OECD), have also raised the attention, granting ICTs with the task to achieve strategic urban development goals, such as sustainability and improving the quality of life of the citizens (OECD – EUROSTAT, 2005). Similarly, many cities have used the 'smart city' term to profile themselves as prosperous and well-endowed, in a variety of circumstances: For instance, the Amsterdam Smart City initiative emphasizes the importance of collaboration between the citizens, government and businesses to develop smart projects that will 'change the world' by saving energy; the Southampton City Council uses smart cards to stress the importance of integrated e-services (e.g. bus passes) (Caragliu et al., 2009); the City of Edinburgh Council has formed a smart city vision around an action plan for government transformation and the Malta Smart City promotes a Business Park to achieve more economic growth. IBM, Siemens and ORACLE have formed their visions as well. A number of EU research and policy project have emerged also to deal with various issues of the 'smart city'. A recently concluded pan-European research project IntelCities (2009) for example concluded that governance, as a process and outcome of joint decision-making and action, has a leading role to play in building the 'smart city' and that cities should develop collaborative digital environments to boost local competitiveness and prosperity by using knowledge networks and partnerships, integrated e-services and governance (Paskaleva, 2009). A present Smart Cities INTERREG project (2011) is using an innovation network between cities and academic partners

to develop and deliver better e-services in the North Sea Region through novel co-design processes. This follows a 2009 Smart Cities Future Conference in Manchester (UK) which endorsed open innovation and effective collaboration between stakeholders as the critical factors for 'starting the journey towards the future "smart city"'.

Yet, as only recently Hollands (2008) has revealed, cities all too often claim to be smart, but without defining what this means, or offering the evidence to support such claims. Moreover, smart-er cities appear to be simply 'wired cities', though 'progressive(ly) smart[er] cities must seriously start with people and the human capital side of the equation, rather than blindly believing that IT itself can automatically transform and improve cities' (2008, p.315). And as he goes on to conclude 'the critical factor in any successful community, enterprise, or venture, is its people and how they interact' (2008, p.306). It is around this viewpoint that smart cities can be progressive because they use digital technologies not to hardwire themselves but to be socially-inclusive, foster good governance and create better services that improve the quality of life of the citizens, with an outlook to long-term sustainability and competitiveness, from which the current study sets forth.

Taking the above vision forward, the article reflects upon the current trends and understanding of what it means for urban administrations, policy makers and businesses in Europe for cities to be smart and what it takes them to become smart-er in the future. The role of the 'smart city' as a nexus for open innovation is of special attention as this theme and strategy have become focal in present discussions among the Member States about the Future of Internet, Living Labs (LLs) and Innovation and Competitiveness-driven (Urban) Development. By conducting a critical review of some high-profile programmes and initiatives on smart cities, the emerging trends are explored and insights are drawn about the challenges and the pathways to the 'smart-er city'. The analysis is based on four Smart Cities projects and the relevant EU programmes. They have been chosen for this study because collectively they reveal what the Europeans have entrusted in their 'Smart Cities' strategic outlook. The analysis also responds to the quest of the research and academic communities, as Holland puts it, to identify the defining components, critical insights and institutional means by which to get beyond the self-congratulatory ideas of smart cities.

The article is structured around five main sections. The Introduction sets out the rational for the study. The second section discusses the relevant research background. The third section presents some major European projects on smart cities. The fourth section follows up with a discussion about the emerging trends and draws insights about the driving stimulus behind building smarter future cities in Europe. The Conclusion sums us the outcomes of the study against its objectives and identifies strategic questions in building the smart city that is sustainable, competitive and inclusive and which is using all the merits of open innovation and society's great potentials.

THEORETICAL BACKGROUND
THE CONCEPT OF THE SMART CITY

In the course of the last decade, the concept of the 'smart city', considered by many as the new century's stage of urban development, has become fairly trendy in the policy and business arenas (Komninos, 2002). Academic interest has grown as well. Mainstream approaches to it tend to deal with issues relevant to the use of ICT in making cities more technologically advanced. Accordingly, the availability and quality of the ICT infrastructure have become the determining factors for many cities to brand themselves as 'smart'. In contrast to this approach, a growing number of late studies suggest that these are the environmental interests and the social capital which drive urban progress nowadays. Factors like the capacity of the human (Berry and

Glaeser, 2005; Glaeser and Berry, 2006), the relational capital (Paskaleva, 2009) and the role of higher education, skills, creativity and talent (Shapiro, 2006; Mellander and Florida, 2009) have emerged as the predominant drivers of cities' evolution. And as local quality of life becomes more and more important in determining population clustering, amongst other modern urban phenomena, the significance of territorial amenities has ultimately become one of the major components of urban attractiveness and development (Rappaport, 2009), towards which progress should be principally measured.

But despite the significant advance in ICT and urban research moving towards beyond technology and city growth fundamentals, the construct of the 'smart city' remains ambiguous and continues to be used in various ways. Recent research carried out by the authors of the current issue for the development of the Wikipedia website on smart cities, has revealed that up until now smart cities have been generally identified along six main dimensions: smart economy; smart mobility; smart environment; smart people; smart living; and smart governance (Wikipedia, 2011). It has also been revealed that the main characteristics of a 'smart city' which have come up in the discussions can be grouped in three main categories:

1 *The level of exploitation of networked infrastructure* to improve economic and political efficiency and enable social, cultural and urban development (Hollands, 2008; Nijkamp, 2008), with the term infrastructure signifying business services, leisure and lifestyle services, housing and ICTs (satellite TVs, mobile and fixed phones, computer networks, e-commerce, internet services (IoS)), and a smart city meaning a wired city as the main development model and of connectivity as the source of growth (Komninos, 2002).

2 *A vision and a strategy for creating the competitive city* with the smart city taking

the opportunities of ICTs to increase local prosperity and competitiveness and approaches varying from stressing the importance of the multi-actor, multi-sector, and multi-level urban perspective towards competitiveness and sustainability (Odendal, 2003; Paskaleva, 2009) to signifying the presence of a creative class, the quality of and dedicated attention to the urban environment, the level of education, multi-modal accessibility, and the use of ICTs for public administration to increase urban wealth (Caragliu et al., 2009), or simply underlining business-led urban development (Hollands, 2008).

3 *An approach to sustainable and inclusive cities*, placing the main weight on the social capital of urban development. Here the smart city knows how to learn, adapt and innovate (Schuller et al., 2000; Coe et al., 2001) and the focus could be social inclusion in public services (e.g. Southampton's smart card) (Southampton City Council, 2006) or involving the citizens in service co-design for better services (Deakin, 2007; Deakin and Allwinkle, 2007). Sustainability, in this sense is considered as the very strategic element of the smart cities and achieving environmental or social sustainability through participation of the public in local decision-making is key to increasing democracy and governance (Caragliu et al., 2009; Deakin, 2010).

But despite the growing attention, definitions or systematic models of the 'smart city' remain scarce and the debate on its principles and strategic policy agenda continues to be unresolved. At the same time, cities are continuing to grow, urban infrastructure and resources are becoming more scarce, and the state of the urban environment is determining most people's quality of life, which suggests that urban evolution should be driven by clear agendas about the future-oriented sustainable cities. Understanding the factors that make cities and urban livelihoods 'smart', yet

sustainable with better quality of life becoming a life-time outcome of urban functioning, appears decisive for the future debates of the 'smart city'.

Although the smart-er city is generally considered an outcome of smart cities practices, this article aims to broaden its scope into looking at the smart city as an 'activator' of change through exploring relevant open innovation processes. With the latter emerging as a powerful driver of this new paradigm shift, no general and explicit attention is yet given to a number of important questions: How open innovation shapes the way cities become smart? To what extent the way in which it operates is 'transformative'? Can open innovation dynamics that generate new communities, organizations and processes? Can help cities cope with the challenges of implementing new technologies everywhere and for everything? Some of these questions have already been raised and many of them have now found their way into EU strategies towards future European society and its cities, but, as yet, few answers have been forthcoming.

THE EU SMART CITIES AGENDA

The Smart Cities theme has emerged in several European programmes but its importance has recently increased in the landscape of the Future Internet (FI), the main argument being that smart cities can serve as a catalyst for FI research, as they form dense social ecosystems that heavily rely on Internet technology and in turn Internet technology and applications heavily influence social interactions. It has been also argued that it is in the smart cities where the initial impact of the FI through their advanced applications will be most visible to European citizens and direct feedback from EU citizens on FI technology and applications can be obtained (Lemke and Luotonen, 2009). As a result of this policy, a number of new initiatives have occurred in the last couple of years such as the FIREBALL and FIRESTATION co-ordination and support actions, the Smart Santander smart-city experimental facility and several smart city pilots funded under the ICT Policy Support Programme (PSP) of the European Commission.

A number of EU programmes have highlighted the importance of the smart city for Europe's Digital Agenda. The i2010 (EC, 2010a) initiative emphasized three main pillars of the Digital Society (i) Developing the Single European Information Space in order to promote an open and competitive internal market for information society and media. (ii) Further strengthening Innovation and Investment in ICT research in order to promote growth and more and better jobs. (iii) Ensuring an Inclusive European Information Society which is consistent with sustainable development and is able to prioritize better public services and quality of life, to develop creative contact across Europe and to improve the efficiency and effectiveness of public services. Following on that, the Directorate General Information Society's Competitiveness and Innovation Programme has launched the ICT PSP Programme for stimulating innovation and competitiveness through the wider uptake and enhanced use of ICTs by citizens, business (particularly small and medium-size enterprises (SMEs)) and government, with which user-driven innovation was linked to Internet-enabled services in the smart cities.

The 'innovation strategy' was is in the heart of i2010 and continues to drive policy activities. The importance of the role played by the end-users in the Digital Society is particularly recognized. But it is clear that as services and applications develop they will need to be sustained through user-driven open innovation in order to be scalable and replicable at a mass-market level. And as user generated content and co-created applications grow exponentially, they will need to be linked to new and innovative business models that will ensure effective implementation and sustainability. Therefore, bringing together FI technologies with LLs methodologies and practices has been chosen as a viable way forward in advancing e-services

(EC, 2010b). However, despite all the efforts during the last fifteen years to improve government services, transactions and interactions with European citizens and businesses, technical and procedural limitations have combined to prevent cities from truly harnessing the full power of ICT to collaborate, create and deliver genuinely 'smarter' citizens- and business-centred services. The current economic crisis combined with growing citizen expectations is placing an increasing pressure on cities to overcome existing barriers and provide better and more efficient infrastructures and e-services. Innovative ICT solutions – particularly those created in the user driven, open innovation environments of LLs – appear to hold an important key to helping European cities resolve this dilemma and work smarter.

Therefore, the new forward looking '2020 Strategy' emphasizes three main types of growth – *smart growth* (fostering knowledge, innovation, education and digital society), *sustainable growth* (making our production more resource efficient while boosting our competitiveness) and *inclusive growth* (raising participation in the labour market, the acquisition of skills and the fight against poverty) (EC, 2010c). The present discussion anticipates the three key goals of Europe 2020 for *smart, sustainable and inclusive growth* and in particular the key area where progress is mostly needed – innovation. The latter has been taken up by the late EU commitment to support the development of LLs as an environment for open innovation. The European Network of Living Labs demonstrates the desire of the LLs cities to share their experience in Europe and globally. National and regional level networking of LLs is also increasingly taking place, for example, in UK, Belgium and Finland. The main idea of the LL concept, on which this article builds, is keeping the users continuously involved in making better products and services while their expectations are continuously monitored and reflected upon in a systematic process.

Other EU programmes are also influencing the smart city agenda. On a spatial scale, the Lisbon and Gothenburg strategies are closely relevant to it by aiming to take advantage of emerging FI technologies to achieve competitiveness and sustainability in a complementary symbiosis rather than as a trade-off. The Territorial Agenda, URBACT Programme and the Leipzig Urban Charter, place a particular emphasis on cities and emphasize the need to build on their potentials as centres of knowledge and sources of growth and innovation and their unique cultural and architectural qualities to address all dimensions of sustainable development at the same time and with the same weight. On a sectoral level, the FI Initiative aims to redesign the Internet, taking a broad multi-disciplinary approach, to meet Europe's societal and commercial ambitions. Together these programmes are shaping the future of the 'smart city' agenda.

THE ROLE OF OPEN INNOVATION IN THE SMART CITY

Although the ideas and discussions date back to the early 1960s, it was Henry Chesbrough in 2003 who first promoted the idea of 'open innovation', a paradigm that assumes that firms can and should use external ideas as well as internal ideas, and internal and external paths to market, as they look to advance their technology. Most recent debates, however, suggest that 'open innovation' should not just refer to industry but also to the ways government and other institutions work and collaborate with society (Chesbrough et al., 2006). This emerging notion of open innovation, based on networking and inter-institutional relations appears highly relevance to the paradigm of the 'smart city' that is anticipated in the present study.

As the critique of the predominantly technology-driven approach to smart cities is increasing, there is a strong need to align innovation policies with the goals of urban development. Smart cities also require 'smart citizens' if they are to be truly inclusive, innovative and sustainable. The promise of the information society to create new ways of empowering people to play a fuller and more equal role in emerging governance systems through their access to dynamic Internet enabled services, is also proving to be a big challenge, as not everyone is getting equal access to the skills and opportunities that are supposed to be there. Previous EU initiatives, particularly those focusing on e-government and e-inclusion, have tackled the 'digital divide' only to find that the persistent inequalities blighting many urban neighbourhoods mitigate against citizen empowerment and participation within the information society. This calls for a new approach in which the focus is first and foremost on citizen empowerment as an essential catalyst in creating a new paradigm to transform the dynamics of data flows, management and service development towards the smart city.

The potential of new bottom-up approaches based on user-generated content, social media and Web 2.0 applications opens up vast possibilities for a new interpretation and understanding of spatial differences and local effects, seen through the experiences of the citizens themselves, leading to new forms of empowerment for those citizens. The latter has the potential to enable citizens to build the social capital and capacity required to become co-creators and co-producers of new and innovative services with the means to ensure that they are delivered in more effective and inclusive ways, taking full advantage of new Internet-based technologies and applications (Cahn, 2001).

Developing collaborative processes between local 'smart citizens', government and developer communities will evidently support and enhance the process, which brings up the idea of 'co-production' of goods and services as core to 'open innovation' for the 'smart-er city'. Amidst the most recent crisis of reform of public services in the UK, a ground-breaking National Endowment for Science Technology and the Arts (NESTA) report (Boyle and Harris, 2009) went on to reveal that 'co-production' offers a new way for citizens to share not just in the design but also in the delivery of services and contribute their own wisdom and experience in ways that can broaden and strengthen services and make them more effective. As a result, co-production is developing as a practical agenda for system change in the UK, based on four key principles:

1 recognizing people as assets
2 valuing work differently
3 promoting reciprocity
4 building social networks.

Forming partnerships between professionals and the public, yet again appears crucial for improving the effectiveness and efficiency of local services. Establishing systematic and long-term collaboration between front line practitioners and developers can help create a more positive environment for 'co-production' of local services but in policymaking as well to make the system more responsive to community needs. The Internet-based technologies and e-services provide endless opportunities for stimulating 'co-production'. In return, the latter can provide new opportunities for securing citizens' engagement and active involvement in the process of developing 'smart services' which can help to accelerate the uptake of these technologies and services. This 'virtuous circle' is then capable of enhancing cities' ability to grow and sustain 'innovation ecosystems' and, through this, to develop more inclusive, higher quality and efficient services. The added value for the users is that they have a real incentive to become more involved as co-producers, as well as users, of the content and services available in the emerging smart city through having access to new skills, employment possibilities and better quality of life. It is these possibilities which can then make these approaches more sustainable, by embedding the pro-active involvement of citizens in all

aspects of designing and delivering services and thus providing both citizens and the public authorities responsible for providing these services with a new rationale to make the Public-Private-People Partnership (PPPP) an approach which is viable and desirable in the smart city (SMARTiP, 2010).

USING THE LLS APPROACH FOR SMART CITY INNOVATION

Innovation policies that support and foster innovation processes strategically are perceived crucial for increasing urban competitive advantages in the future. For ICT innovations in particular, more open and networked forms of collaboration between industrial, governmental, academic and user stakeholders in the innovation process has been identified as a serious policy challenge. Yet, experience has shown that such open or networked innovation should not be interpreted in terms of a naive or ideology-driven concept, but rather in terms of a concrete solution for dealing with complex and systemic innovation of ICT products and services that are composed of many complementary components, as well as for dealing with the fundamental unpredictability of ICT usage. At this background, the LL approach has grown rapidly in Europe as an outgrowth of William J. Mitchell original concept at the beginning of this Century of involving city dwellers more actively in urban planning and city design (Mitchell, 2005).

The LL is seen as a platform for implementing an open innovation model to pilot different initiatives towards the Europe 2020 perspective of well-being and sustainability. The LLs are commonly defined as user-driven innovation ecosystems based on a business–citizens–government partnership which enables users to take active part in the research, development and innovation process (EC, 2010d). Partners include cities, municipalities, innovation agencies, universities, large industrial partners, SMEs, citizens and so on. Benchmark examples of LLs are environments in which technology is given shape in real life contexts and in which (end) users are considered 'co-producers' (Ballon et al., 2007; Jensen, 2007). An ecosystem is established in which new products and services are created, prototyped and used in real-time environments. Thus, users are not treated as object in the innovation process or as mere customers, but as early stage contributors and innovators (Wise and Høgenhaven, 2008).

Since 2006, LLs have rapidly grown throughout Europe. Networking activities have been also established to share principles and best practices and some national and European projects (including Laboranova, Ecospace and C@R) have explored issues dealing with creating awareness, developing tools and methods, as well as learning from best practices. The European Network of Living Labs (ENOLL, 2010) has been in the center of this new movement among the cities, which in 2010 had 250 LLs across Europe on both the inter-regional level (e.g. Nordic-Baltic Network of Living Labs) as well on the national level (Italian Network of Living Labs, Finnish Network of Living Labs and UK Network of Living Labs). Recent efforts have also shifted towards using the results of this cross-border collaboration to connect smart cities but the question of how can open innovation become a true and effective instrument for making cities smart-er remains a challenge. Core to finding the adequate solutions, as the previous discussion has shown, seems designing and adopting a smart city model on which cities can become smarter, sustainable and inclusive, in a systematic and cohesive way. The following analysis attempts to shed light on the approach by exploring open innovation as a key driver of the 'smart city' taken as a LL ecosystem.

SMART CITY TRENDS IN EUROPE

This section focuses on the main approaches and objectives of four recently launched policy support projects in Europe. The analysis aims to show how ideas and strategies are being strategically shaped across the areas of smart cities, FI and LLs.

THE SMARTIP PROJECT: SMART METROPOLITAN AREAS REALIZED THROUGH INNOVATION AND PEOPLE

SMARTiP builds on the philosophy that developing 'smart citizens' within a network of 'smart cities' can be an important catalyst for 'smart growth', one that will curb the inequalities in smart citizens and public services. Headed by the Manchester Digital Development Agency, this 13-partner initiative takes a holistic approach to e-government to tackle various inter-connected policy agendas simultaneously and address the need for smarter redistribution and service design as well as recognition of the role of people in achieving it in a sustainable and fairer way. It is assumed as a starting point, that socio-economic disadvantage goes hand in hand with what has been termed the 'digital divide' and therefore argued that access to the Internet, or what is sometimes termed 'networks of opportunity' (Graham and Marvin, 1996) is a basic requirement for full realization of citizens' economic, social and political participation in a democratic society (Mossberger et al., 2008). Thus the incentive to widen access to technology, particularly in areas of deprivation, seems highly justified. As it is clear that without sufficient demand for online services from all strata of society, the cost benefits rooted in ICT-driven automation cannot be unlocked (SMARTiP DoW, 2010).

Despite the progress in e-government, it has been widely acknowledged that the promise of the 'democratizing' and 'empowering' impacts of networked ICTs has still not been fully realized and there still is a fundamental gap between vision and delivery of government e-services. Among other things, the casting of the 'citizen' as a 'customer' has hampered more creative developments in government-citizen relationships. And while the public sector is yet to fully exploit the opportunities offered by online technologies, 'web 2.0' has taken internet users, private individuals as well as businesses, by storm. What is key to 'all things 2.0' is that individuals drive the content development, they broadcast, share and consume content of their own choosing and often creation. For government, there is no clear or coherent strategy yet for the use of web 2.0. Instead, a raft of initiatives has emerged incrementally, seeking to 'crowd-source' public policy, or to connect with citizens via online platforms. Recent examples of this are two centrally run campaigns in the UK: 'Show us a better way' – to hear your ideas for new products that could improve the way public information is communicated (UK Cabinet Office, 2008) and 'Building Democracy' to support projects developing new ways to help people participate in public discussions and influence government policy (UK Ministry of Justice, 2008). Going beyond notions of value for money, the social inclusion agenda referred to in the SMARTiP project opens up an important dimension to what technology should be harnessed for by local government. The argument made is that democratic participatory values should be incorporated into service technologies adopted by local government. While web 2.0 is diverse and it can encompass all forms of participation, facilitating smarter design of public services, as well as offering recognition of residents' own concerns remains key to the challenges ahead. It is about building a local on-line presence, an enhanced sense of place and improving services in ways which help to reduce spatial inequalities that will drive the smart city agenda in the future.

Therefore, creating a digital community with smart citizens and smart developers is the main instrument for achieving the goals to create new, dynamic relationships in the smart city. The common interests can be drawn from any area of the digital and non-digital world. SMARTiP aims to build the 'bridges' needed to connect 'digital communities' together, enabling developers and citizens to find

dynamic and imaginative ways to interact and to build wider 'communities of interest' drawing inspiration and experience from the open source community and the social economy world. The projects is based on the experience gained from digital communities in Manchester with the Manchester Living Lab, building upon the work being undertaken to create cross-border collaboration, through specific projects such as APOLLON and more generally through ENoLL. The new process of co-production is employed across the three main themes (i) smart engagement; (ii) smart environments and (iii) smart mobility (Figure 1).

As a result, SMARTiP will advance developments in several cross-cutting policy lines – smart cities who need smart citizens, innovation driven by the users, service co-creation and co-production, user involvement as producers, empowering citizens to become part of the innovation process, adequate social capital for the FI and new innovative business models to support implementation. The main mechanisms to achieve this is building new collaborations so cities can understand innovation, innovators can understand cities and citizens can in turn become really engaged and users who are not merely content providers, but both the producers and delivers of services. It is anticipated thus that a long-term collaboration

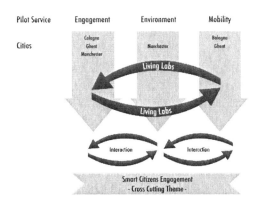

FIGURE 1 SMARTiP pilots focus and methodology

between Smart cities will be achieved, raising the profile of LLs and FI methodologies, creating open 'citizen developer' communities, establishing PPPPs, co-production in the design and delivery of services, and transferable applications and services with adequate business models (Carter, 2010). The projects involves a cross-disciplinary team of five city regions – Manchester, Gent, Oulu, Bologna/Emilia Romagna and Cologne – technology developers, Living Labs, the University of Manchester and a locally based NGO Peoples Voice Media.

PERIPHÈRIA: NETWORKED SMART PERIPHERAL CITIES FOR SUSTAINABLE LIFESTYLES

Periphèria's main goal is to deploy convergent FI platforms and services for the promotion of sustainable lifestyles in and across emergent networks of 'smart' peripheral cities in Europe, dynamic realities of the big cities with a specific capacity for green creativity. Its Open Service Convergence Platform, an 'Internet by and for the People', assumes a Social Information Architecture, integrating sensor networks, real time three-dimensional (3D) and mobile location-based services with the FI paradigms of Internet of Things (IoT), Internet of Services and Internet of People (IoP). Specific technologies – results of previous research initiatives, emerging devices and platforms and ad hoc mash-ups designed and implemented on the spot – come together to converge into a common LL-like setting for the co-creation of next-generation personal and collective services (Periphèria, 2010).

At the heart of the Periphèria convergent platform model is social interaction, which occurs at the 'run-time' moments in which the infrastructures and services are jointly and dynamically discovered, invoked and composed. User-generated content is considered the main driver of social interaction, with the latter occurring in different urban settings and conditions. Taking this notion forward, the five project pilots –

(i) user-generated media for inter-cultural dialogue and civic interaction (Malmo, Sweden); (ii) traffic and transportation-related information (Bremen, Germany); (iii) strategic planning (Athens, Greece); (iv) cultural and natural heritage (Genoa, Italy) and (v) e-government services to citizens and businesses (Palmela, Portugal) – are designed to analyse developments across diverse cultural, institutional and territorial frameworks. The key belief is that convergence of FI platforms occurs through social interaction in concrete situations, in an 'Internet by and for the People' which is a discovery-driven rather than functionalities-driven centripetal aggregation of the main FI paradigms:

- The *Internet of things* as the ambient mobile-enabled infrastructure of sensors and connectivity that is fully networked and context-aware.
- The *Internet of services* as the service-oriented environments that finally break away from functional logics approach to embrace a participatory, smart gaming and simulation approach to service discovery and provision.
- The *Internet of people* as the emergent social architectures of relations, transactions and

FIGURE 2 Periphèria's Future Internet Concept

learning, using semantics of time and place as well as semantics of inter-personal situations (Figure 2).

The LL approach is assumed to shift technology research and development (R&D) out of the laboratory and into the real world in a systemic blend of technological with social innovation. This occurs through a 're-negotiation' of specific city infrastructures (named 'Urblets') and patterns of behaviour (named 'Behavlets') driven by FI possibilities through serious games. The five archetypical 'Arenas' – specific urban settings or innovation playgrounds, with defined social features and infrastructure requirements – are the spaces where co-design and service integration processes unfold:

1 *Smart neighbourhood*: where media-based social interaction occurs
2 *Smart street*: where new transportation behaviours develop
3 *Smart square*: where civic decisions are taken
4 *Smart museum and park*: where natural and cultural heritage feed learning
5 *Smart city hall*: where mobile e-government services are delivered.

A 12-partner team headed by Alfamicro Sistema de Computadores Lda (Portugal) is carrying out the project, putting together industry and research experts with five city administrations from Europe.

EUROPEAN PLATFORM FOR INTELLIGENT CITIES: DELIVERING EFFECTIVE SMART CITY SERVICES ACROSS EUROPE

European Platform for Intelligent Cities (EPIC) combines innovation ecosystem processes, e-government service applications and new cloud computing technologies to create a scalable and flexible pan-European platform – The EPIC for innovative, user-driven public service delivery through user-driven open

innovation, connected smart cities and web-based advanced services. The EPIC platform combines latest technologies, from a semantic engine, 3D Geo-locating to the FI, to provide new tools and possibilities to existing cityinnovation ecosystems to enhance their R&D process and enable them to deliver 'smarter' city services. This will enable (i) local SME's to rapidly prototype scalable new user-driven solutions; (ii) innovative public administrations to test and deploy them and (iii) cities across Europe to ultimately access and use them. By providing access to a market-leading shared infrastructure that facilitates rapid prototyping and testing, EPIC aims to drive innovation forward. The EPIC service platform combines city applications leveraging LLs and smart cities service delivery innovations, such as Relocation Service, Urban Planning Service and Smart Environment Service to implement the new Intelligent Cities platform.

The idea is to reach out to cities, LLs, businesses and other stakeholders to collaborate in accelerating innovation and smart service delivery. The hypothesis is that cities will be able to become 'smarter' if they utilize the EPIC Platform. A roadmap will guide their efforts for improving service delivery to achieve the benefits of 'smart' working. LLs methodology is used for testing and validating 'Apple iPhone' services thorough engaging the citizens, SMEs and cities to plug existing and new co-designed web-based services into the open EPIC platform so that aspiring cities like Tirgu Mures in Romania can easily connect to the platform and use them. The added value to cities and LLs will be a new 'smart' service delivery infrastructure in a scalable and cost-efficient manner with an easy access to innovative new applications from across Europe. To the citizens and business, it will be the increasing desire to access localized, user-centred government services jointly with other private sector offerings, that is, quicker, faster and more personalized. Fifteen EU partners from industry, city administration, universities and LLs, among which Manchester City Council, IBM, Fraunhofer Institute FKIE, ENoLL, Deloitte Consulting, National Technical University of Athens and others, have joined efforts in the next 2 years, headed by IBBT, Brussels (Ballon, 2010).

PEOPLE: PILOT SMART URBAN ECOSYSTEMS LEVERAGING OPEN INNOVATIONS FOR PROMOTING AND ENABLING E-SERVICES

The PEOPLE project aims to accelerate the uptake of smart cities through an advanced deployment and uptake of innovative internet-based services in order to help them provide a better quality of life for their citizens; by applying user-driven open innovation methodologies and processes. Four pilot smart open innovation urban ecosystems (PEOPLE Pilots, 2010) are created to showcase the benefits for cities of growing smarter and more sustainable, using ICT services. Establishing a social network for the PEOPLE Pilots for future 'Smart Open Innovation Urban Ecosystems' and modelling activities for appraising user attributes for the identification of new service opportunities are key methodological instruments. Smart mobility and urban information management scenarios are used to develop the new e-services related to public safety information and urban living in the areas of commerce, leisure and tourism. PEOPLE's key philosophy is that social networks and integration of e-services are fundamental to building the smart city. It is suggested therefore that networking ICT services should be developed to enhance co-existence, focusing on various areas of the city life and the real needs of the local stakeholders.

PEOPLE uses an open data model and flows of information to develop the new internet-based services which are integrated, composed and deployed from various data coming from the urban ecosystem. Four project's pilots are carried out: (i) Bilbao (Spain) focuses on public safety and city living's aspects of quality-of-life information services; (ii) Vitry sur Seine (France) deals with public safety and mobility information particular to groups in risk of exclusion, both in terms of social life and business opportunities; (iii) Thermi (Greece) creates an 'Intelligent City Centre' to provide information around commerce, leisure and tourism and (iv) Bremen (Germany) uses the Technology Park and the University to develop new services about campus life according to the needs of the specific users – students, researchers, visiting experts and companies. Eight service applications are being developed to, together; sustain the identity of the area that combines innovation and commercial activities, so innovation is thus taken as an entertaining activity. ANOVA IT Consulting (Italy) is leading the project; including eight other partners from Spain, France, Greece and Germany (Del Rozo, 2010).

DISCUSSION

It is clear that the EU agenda is strategically moving beyond the IT paradigm of the 'smart city'. Despite the broad and dynamic mixture of visions and approaches; however, the theme continues to attract the attention of many different sectors and professionals. The most important insight that is coming from the analysis of the current trends is that to meet the complex challenges of the future cities, society should use the benefits of the modern ICT-technology and the full capacity of the urban communities to provide better services and goods to the public, bringing together government, citizens and the private entrepreneurs. But to bring this complex agenda forward, new and consistent 'smart city' strategies are necessary, ones that can contribute to achieving urban sustainability and better quality of the life for the general citizen.

With the advance of technologies, society's spirit of innovation is booming. Open innovation is emerging as the new paradigm for building the 'smart city'. With it, government and developers can draw on the expertise, skills, and knowledge of the citizens to develop advanced services and goods that are relevant to the needs of the people and the urban environment. Through open innovation the boundaries between firms, society and government open up to transfer innovation inwards and outwards in the urban ambiance and beyond, to boost research, development and delivery through partnerships and other means of facilitation. Open innovation in the smart city thus becomes part of a much broader shift that is emerging across different sectors and city networks, and most visibly between the public, private, and voluntary sectors. Central to this move is a new process of co-production which understandingly calls for new models of production and consumption, which Murray has defined as 'distributed networks to sustain and manage relationships', such that blur the boundaries between producers and consumers, underline systematic informal interactions and entail a strong capacity of shared values, abilities and capacities. And with more and more networking and collaborative initiatives on local and international level, the conditions are beginning to emerge that are likely to accelerate open innovation in the future. But to move forward to a new scale, a new logic, principles and agendas for the smart city are necessary to evolve.

From the present critical review of how smart cities are linked to and are dependent on open innovation, five main directions for moving forwards have emerged, and these are a useful guide to the next steps for open innovation too.

1 Raising social interaction in the heart of the smart city model, in which the infrastructures and services are jointly and dynamically discovered, invoked and composed by providers and users alike.
2 Creating open 'digital citizen-developer' communities and establishing PPPPs to find dynamic and imaginative ways to interact and create, drawing inspiration and experience from open innovation and sustainable urban development.

3 Building new collaborations and networks so cities can understand innovation, innovators understand cities, citizens to become effectively engaged and users to become content and service producers and deliverers.
4 Deploying convergent FI platforms and services for the promotion of sustainable life and work styles in and across emergent networks of 'smart' cities.
5 Creating smart open innovation urban ecosystems – specific urban settings or innovation playgrounds which combine innovation, and social and commercial activities to enable open innovation and showcase the benefits for localities of growing smarter and more sustainable.

This course of development is consistent with the emerging political argument about sharing the potentials of innovation in the digital economy, despite the fact that cities articulate different 'open innovation' approaches and 'smart city' objectives. Notwithstanding the wide-ranging rhetoric, what is really missing in the current discussion about the 'smart city', yet comes out as a critical factor in future urban development, is the acknowledgment of the special role of the territory in providing the opportunity and the resources for the flourishing of open innovation. As many non-technological studies and policy initiatives have shown, the physical amenities of the place, its people and their culture matter a great deal for the future sustainable city. This means that open innovation too has a geographical locus. The present analysis has visibly shown that open innovation in the smart city is strongly embedded locally in spite taking the advantages of networking with other cities and communities. Therefore, capturing the true values of the territory and its total capacity – socio-economic, environmental, cultural and ICT – that is consciously and strategically geared towards improving urban sustainability, governance and the urban quality of life – stands up as the greatest challenge ahead. In this line of thoughts, one working definition that comes out of the present review is that *open innovation in smart cities means using ICT for delivering more sustainable and inclusive cities with better quality of life for their citizens through delivering better services and goods in a mutual and creative relationship between local officials, professionals, and the people, supported by the right set of strategic policies*. This implies that open innovation is not only a mindful but also strategically driven collaboration between the stakeholders, which leads to a systematic change in the way cities grow smart.

A number of agents are key to the transformations. The human capital is in the heart of the process. Whether people are currently defined as users, clients, or citizens, they all provide the vital ingredients which allow innovation to flourish and to be more effective. As urban challenges continue to grow, it seems perfectly logical to ask people for their help and to use their capacities in building their 'smart-er' city. Open innovation can offer the opportunity to transform the dynamic of the 'smart city' by pooling the many types of skills and knowledge of the people, based on their lived experience and professional learning. This understanding is central for the idea of open innovation in the 'smart city'. This implies, however, that the production and delivery of services and goods should be turned inside out, so cities can truly rediscover the potentials of the people and re-invigorate the social networks of their communities. Because open innovation goes beyond the idea of citizens' engagement in the urban affairs and implies fostering new principles of mutual partnership, not just public and private but this time PPPPs. Therefore, people should be recognized as assets and all their work that makes the city more sustainable and more socially just should be valued.

It is obvious that what these ambitions have in common is the shift in attitude to the users of the urban services and the potentials of the

citizenry in their localities to bring change. The latter have the true potential to become an effective instrument for implementing open innovation not just locally but in collaboration with other global actors, technologies and platforms. The outcome of this, where it happens, can be a radical shift of the nature and focus of the city services, for example – not just looking at the needs of the people, but increasingly looking outwards to the potentials of the people in their concrete territory – the local neighbourhoods or street, the city centre or park, the urban government or the larger region. This analysis has clearly shown that open innovation provides the alternative to rejuvenate the local potentials of the territory, where citizens are consciously aware of and make the choice to share the responsibilities and the impacts of the process of co-living, co-production and co-decision as part of urban sustainable development. It is thus the concept of the territory with its assets – physical, human and cultural – combined with the paradigms of sustainability, governance and strategic planning which is likely to drive future developments in the area.

Another important insight of this review is the transformation of the traditional model of public service development – consisting generally of design, production, delivery and, ideally evaluation – towards an 'outward' looking service development where the adequacy and the viability of the urban services is safeguarded by the people's involvement in all stages of the process and the relevant activities (Figure 3).

As literature research shows, only few studies have examined service development in the public sphere so far and models for the development of service-systems, in comparison to models for product development, are rare (Tan et al., 2004). Service development studies can be typically found in marketing research in the financial, insurance and health care industries (Alam and Perry, 2002). Generally, models for service development derive from existing models of product development, but research in service

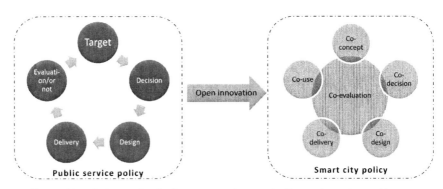

FIGURE 3 The transition of urban service development towards a sustainable open innovation model

sphere emphasises the difference – products are 'things' and services are 'processes'. Recent service-oriented perspectives emphasise the importance of the customer relationships and on-going need satisfaction (Johns, 1999).

Yet, while traditional service development models seek to describe the complete chain of activities, our open innovation service model suggests a systematic approach for structuring development phases collaboratively with the users, creating overlap and interaction between them in order to improve the overall service development performance (Edvardsson, 2005). The focus is on both the process and the product – the development of the specific service – aligned with the users' activities and demands. Thus, with this new model approach we create a dependency between co-creation of concepts, design, production, delivery, and use with a self-sustained co-evaluation process, all of which involve a close integration of activities, tactically and strategically – with regard to the overall Smart City Policy agenda. We expand the development model in phases, so that it also encompasses the concept development and use phases to ensure continuous development that is aligned with the user's preferences and demands. This outward looking open innovation service model means new roles and responsibilities. A key difference in our approach is that the urban citizen is a key part in the entire service life period. It also means new relationships;

typically, a public service provision is derived (top-down) from national and local targets. Our approach attempts to uncover new relationships and different networks of stakeholders. Here innovation will depend upon both the top-down and the bottom-up approaches based on the new knowledge and creativity of the citizens and their context.

The LL can provide the natural ecosystem for the processes of open innovation. By merging research and innovation processes with the daily, local, real-life context, close to people in their role as both citizens and consumers, using the LL approach can enable the smart city to become a real nexus of open innovation, enabling it to tackle issues of behavioural change and innovation, building appropriate business models, organizational processes and structures, multi-stakeholder participation, nd taking into account (multi-) cultural specifics. It can also broaden the scope and role of open innovation within the EU smart city agenda, providing an essential link between sustainability-oriented urban growth and the competitiveness-driven ICT development, reaching towards the collective goal of territorial cohesion and integration. Yet practice so far has centred primarily on methods, processes and products. Participatory services and co-production of new research in the search of new ways of engaging with the users and the social networks are the latest foci. But it is also clear that a new dimension of open innovation is vital for the 'smart city', this being the importance of open innovation for strategic policy. While their advance is admirable, LLs have not themselves advance better policy governance for the simple yet obvious fact that – to date – they have been not included the citizens in the co-creation of policy. While they helped encourage greater interaction between citizens and civil servants, they have not yet delivered improved governance of location and context based policies for public services. Instead, under the existing LL model civil servants engage with citizens much like private sector engage with customers – that is as end-users to provide input into largely pre-determined new product concepts and designs or, in the case of the public sector, service models. What has been missing in this traditional equation is the pro-active engagement of the users, as citizens, in the shaping and creation of the initial policy direction that ultimately determines service priorities. As the LLs innovation instrument matures it is paramount to ensure this policy dimension is further developed.

CONCLUSION

Building on cross-fertilization of state of the art concepts and approaches and on-going activities and programmes in Europe, the main goal of the current article was to explore the perspectives lying behind the question of whether the smart city is a nexus of open innovation. To find answers, the study looked at the smart city dynamics as an enabler of social interaction, service transformation, governance and territorial rejuvenation as means for cities to become smarter, yet more sustainable, inclusive and attractive to people and businesses. There is considerable evidence that Europe is creating a smart city approach which has become open innovation–driven, but has yet to develop the levers it needs to enable more effective implementation of the strategies. Current trends show that smart cities initiatives are designed to foster primarily FI development and the growth of the LLs to tackle issues of ICT service and product enhance. Given the current diversity of uses of both the smart city and open innovation terms, this article also explains that in the context of the smart city open innovation means co-production and co-delivery of not just goods and services but polices as well. The emerging insights help to increase the understanding of smart cities as nodes for open innovation and how open innovation can itself be applied to build the smart-er city that is more inclusive, have smarter citizens and provides better outcome-looking urban services, which account for what people can do and how, in partnerships with different communities. All things said, the article reveals that the smart city and open innovation are dynamically interrelated – the former provides the ecosystem necessary; the latter boosts the city to become smarter. It is also shown, why, if properly understood and systematically applied open innovation is set yet to create a radical shift in building more sustainable cities, which ultimately translates in more urban governance and resilience of the territory.

But there is a more fundamental problem which is barely addressed by current debates – the policy of building the smart city, in part because of the lack of radically new approaches inherent in existing LLs practices. With most efforts focusing on smart cities activities without understanding the key constructs and principles, it is clear that open innovation can be stalled if a new and cohesive policy approach is not built. Collaboration too is to be re-organized in ways that are more effective and lasting, yet the models and the policies are still not there for what cities are trying to achieve. Dealing with the linked challenges across the stakeholders can affect their ability to change. But making a policy choice towards open innovation around or within a specific urban territory, termed by Peripheria as 'Arena', where it all comes together and as a self-organized system of people, is also necessary. Evidently, this new territorial approach to open innovation in the smart city has to become part of the LL approach too and in the methods, processes and developments it uses. These hand in hand with a new trust in co-production and co-delivery, and enthusiasm about the role of mutual collaboration, social networks and PPPPs.

The current discussion poses another central question – what makes open innovation, as a complexity and wide scale process, and as a continuing and respectful relationship between supportive co-producers – boost the smart city. It is evident that delivering open innovation means cutting the link between people, government and particularly important the voluntary sector. The citizens' demand, the move towards co-production processes at the front office, the need to shift from the user needs to what they can actually contribute – thus to empower the user as citizens' – are all questions that need to find innovative solutions by government and the other stakeholders. Encouraging learning and behaviour change seems the natural way forward. The growing social networks can too support the transition. But open innovation also requires new principally new kinds of urban services so the question arises – can urban government be reconstituted so that co-production reform of services becomes part of the institutional change? One conclusion that comes out of this analysis is that transformation does not necessarily mean new government organizations and structures but adopting innovative, flexible and open processes and mechanism at the front end to enable co-production of services and goods in the city.

Yet, the nature of open innovation is more drastic than this – it is also about using people to remake the way government works which in turn requires a new sustainable governance model of smart city development. It also implies that building the smart city of the future will mean getting on board a mutually rewarding and respectful relationship with the citizens, other professionals, the social communities and other doers to co-participate to build both local and global relationships. To be fair, the citizens and other communities are not yet aware of their own potential, so building bridges with the practitioners and the policymakers is vital for the change. On the EU level, understanding and addressing the key issues of open innovation strategically, means embracing a common definition of open innovation in the smart city and defining the strategy, mainstreaming the policy integration and identifying the areas of urban development where it can have the most profound effect. Embracing the culture of open innovation and the means for utilizing the appropriate measures by the cities is equally important. But building the field further requires first and foremost establishing new communities of city officials and active citizens and professionals whose aspirations for smarter and more sustainable cities can be equalled by their grasp of current and strategic developments as well as their practical skills and knowledge.

REFERENCES

Alam, I., Perry, C., 2002, 'A customer-oriented new service development process', *Journal of Services Marketing* **16**(6), 515–534.

Amsterdam Smart City [available at www.amsterdamsmartcity.nl/#/en].

Ballon, P., 2010, 'Introducing EPIC: European Platform for Intelligent Cities', *Presentation made at the Smart Cities Cluster Meeting*, Brussels, 15 September.

Ballon, P., Pierson, J., Delaere, S., 2007, 'Fostering innovation in networked communications: test and experimentation platforms for broadband systems', in: S.B. Heilesen, S. Siggaard (eds), *Designing for Networked Communications – Strategies and Development*, IDEA, Hershey, PA/London, 137–166.

Berry, C.R., Glaeser, E.L., 2005, 'The divergence of human capital levels across cities', *Regional Science* **84**(3), 407–444.

Boyle, D., Harris, M., 2009, 'The challenge of co-production: how equal partnerships between professionals and the public are crucial to improving public services', New Economic Foundation (NEF), The Lab, NESTA, London.

Cahn, E., 2001, *No More Throwaway People: The Co-production Imperative*, Essential Books, Washington, DC.

Caragliu, A., Del Bo, C., Nijkamp, P., 2009, 'Smart cities in Europe'. *Serie Research Memoranda 0048* (VU University Amsterdam, Faculty of Economics, Business Administration and Econometrics) [available at http://ideas.repec.org/p/dgr/vuarem/2009-48.html].

Carter, D., 2010, SMARTiP: Smart Metropolitan Areas Realised Through Innovation & People [available at http://ec.europa.eu/information_society/activities/livinglabs/docs/smartip_pub.pdf].

Chesbrough, H.W., 2003, *Open Innovation: The New Imperative for Creating and Profiting from Technology*, Harvard Business School Press, Boston.

Chesbrough, H.W., Vanhaverbeke, W., West, J., 2006, *Open Innovation: Researching a New Paradigm*, Oxford University Press, Oxford.

Coe, A., Paquet, G., Roy, J., 2001, 'E-governance and smart communities: a social learning challenge', *Social Science Computer Review* 19(1), 80–93.

Deakin, M., 2007, 'From city of bits to e-topia: taking the thesis on digitally-inclusive regeneration full circle', *Journal of Urban Technology* 14(3), 131–143.

Deakin, M., 2010, 'SCRAN: the SmartCities (inter) regional academic network supporting the development of a trans-national comparator for the standardisation of eGovernment services', in: C. Reddick (ed), *Comparative E-government: An Examination of E-Government Across Countries*, Springer Press, Berlin.

Deakin, M., Allwinkle, S., 2007, 'Urban regeneration and sustainable communities: the role networks, innovation and creativity in building successful partnerships', *Journal of Urban Technology* 14(1), 77–91.

Del Rozo, P., 2010, People Project, CIP Smart Cities Pilot presentation at Helsinki International Conference, 16 November [available at www.slideshare.net/openlivinglabs].

EC, 2010a, i2010 – A European Information Society for growth and employment [available at http://ec.europa.eu/information_society/eeurope/ i2010/index_en.htm].

EC, 2010b, Europe 2020 strategy – Innovation insights from European research in socio-economic sciences, 01 June 2010, Brussels, Belgium [available at http://ec.europa.eu/research/social-sciences/events-107_en.html].

EC, 2010c, Europe 2020, Priorités [available at http://ec.europa.eu/europe2020/priorities/ smart-growth/index_en.htm].

EC, 2010d, Living Labs for user-driven open innovation, Directorate General for the Information Society and Media [available at http://ec.europa.eu/information_society/activities/livinglabs/index_en.htm].

Edvardsson, B., Gustafsson, A., Roos, I., 2005, 'Service portraits in service research: a critical review', *International Journal of Service Industry Management* 16(1), 107–121.

ENoLL, 2010, European Network of Living Labs [available at www.openlivinglabs.eu/aboutus].

Glaeser, E.L., Berry, C.R., 2006, 'Why are smart places getting smarter?', Taubman Cente, Cambridge, MA, Policy Brief, 2006–2.

Graham, S., Marvin, S., 1996, *Telecommunications and the City: Electronic Spaces, Urban Places*, Routledge, London.

Hollands, R.G., 2008, 'Will the real smart city please stand up?', *City* 12(3), 303–320.

IntelCities, 2009 [available at www.intelcitiesproject.com].

Jensen, S. (eds), 2007, *Designing for Networked Communications – Strategies and Development*, IDEA, Hershey, PA/London, 137–166.

Johns, N., 1999, 'What is this thing called service?', *European Journal of Marketing* 33(9), 958–974.

Komninos, N., 2002, *Intelligent Cities: Innovation, Knowledge Systems and Digital Spaces*, Spon Press, London.

Lemke, M., Luotonen, M., 2009, 'Open Innovation for Future Internet-Enabled Services in "Smart" Cities', European Commission, INFSO-F4, Discussion Paper Draft 2.

Mellander, C., Florida, R., 2009, 'Creativity, talent, and regional wages in Sweden', *The Annals of Regional Science* 46(3), 637–660.

Mitchell, W., 2005, *Placing Words: Symbols, Space, and the City*, MIT Press, Cambridge, MA.

Mossberger, K., Tolbert, K., McNeal, R., 2008, *Digital Citizenship: The Internet, Society, and Participation*, MIT Press, Cambridge, MA.

Nijkamp, P., 2008, E pluribus unum. *Research Memorandum, Faculty of Economics*, VU University Amsterdam, Amsterdam.

Odendal, N., 2003, 'Information and communication technology and local governance: understanding the difference between cities in developed and emerging economies', *Computers, Environment and Urban Systems* 27(6), 585–607.

OECD – EUROSTAT, 2005, *Oslo Manual*, OECD – Statistical Office of the European Communities, Paris.

Paskaleva, K., 2009, 'Enabling the smart city: the progress of e-city governance in Europe', *International Journal of Innovation and Regional Development* 1(4), 405–422.

PEOPLE, 2010 [available at www.people-pilot.eu].

Periphèria, 2010, CIP-ICT PSP Call 4 2010 Pilot B: SMARTiP, Description of Work, Confidential document.

Rappaport, J., 2009, 'The increasing importance of quality of life', *Journal of Economic Geography* **9**(6), 779–804.

Schuller, T., Baron, S., Field, J., 2000, 'Social capital: a review and critique', in: S. Baron, J. Field, T. Schuller (eds), *Social Capital: Critical Perspectives*, Oxford University Press, Oxford, 1–38.

Shapiro, J., 2006, 'Smart cities: quality of life, productivity, and the growth effects of human capital', *Review of Economics and Statistics* **88**(2), 324–335.

Smart Cities INTERREG project, 2011 [available at www.smartcities.info/aim].

SMARTiP DoW, 2010, CIP-ICT PSP Call 4 2010 Pilot B: SMARTiP, Description of Work, Confidential document.

Southampton City Council, 2006, Southampton Smartcities Card [available at www.southampton.gov.uk/living/smartcities/], retrieved 12 November 2009.

Tan, A., McAloone, T., Andreasen, M., 2006, 'What happens to integrated product development models with product/service system approaches?' *Proceedings of the 6th Workshop on Integrated Product Development*, in: S. Vajma (ed), Magdeburg, Germany [available at www.ignitiate.com/pdfs/traditional%20PRODUCT%20DEVELOPMENT.pdf].

UK Cabinet office, 2008, Show us a better way Competition [available at http://webarchive.nationalarchives.gov.uk/20100807004350/http://showusabetterway.co.uk].

UK Ministry of Justice, 2008, Building Democracy [available at www.justice.gov.uk/news/newsrelease300708a.htm].

Wikipedia, 2011, Smart City Definition [available at http://en.wikipedia.org/wiki/Smart_city].

Wise, E., Høgenhaven, C., 2008, *User-Driven Innovation*. Research Policy: Oslo.

Intelligent cities: Variable geometries of spatial intelligence

Nicos Komninos

URENIO Research Unit – Aristotle University of Thessaloniki, University Campus, Thessaloniki 54124, Greece

This article discusses the spatial intelligence of cities, the use of information communication technologies (ICTs) and institutional frameworks that support innovation ecosystems of cities and increase the problem-solving capability of communities and cities. It is based on three case studies on Bletchley Park, Cyberport Hong Kong and Smart Amsterdam, which highlight different architectures of spatial intelligence: (1) orchestration intelligence that stems from collaboration within a community and integration of people's skills, know-how, and collective and machine intelligence, (2) amplification intelligence based on learning, up-skilling and talent cultivation using open technology platforms and ICT infrastructure offered by the city, and (3) instrumentation intelligence based on streams of information generated from the functioning of cities, which enable more informed decisions to be taken by citizens and organizations. The article contributes to understanding different processes that make communities more intelligent, and how collective intelligence, people-driven innovation and use of smart devices advance the efficiency, operation and governance of cities.

INTRODUCTION

The starting point for this article was an observation on two types of inflation (in the sense of increased use) related to intelligent cities that occur in contemporary urban development and planning. The first concerns the proliferation of cities that adopt intelligent city strategies and define themselves as smart or intelligent cities. Since 2005, when Urenio Watch (www.urenio.org) began recording developments in the field of innovation ecosystems and intelligent cities, the increasing announcement and diversity of cities adopting intelligent city strategies has

been noted. This has often led to a simplistic use of the terms 'smart' and 'intelligent', which are easily assigned to any digital application associated with cities – often just for marketing purposes – without making clear what intelligence is being improved and how. Hollands (2008) accurately pointed out that urban development in many countries has been increasingly influenced by smart city concepts, but despite the wide use of this urban labelling phenomenon, we know little about so-called smart cities, particularly in terms of what the label both reveals and hides in ideological terms.

The second was an inflation of a different kind, due to the sheer diversification of strategies and digital applications for intelligent cities across the various districts of cities. In our research about the creation of intelligent environments in the city of Thessaloniki, for instance, we found that digital applications useful in different districts of the city (central business district (CBD), port area, university campus, technology districts, etc.) varied substantially (Urenio, 2008). Each district of the city – because of its specialization in manufacturing, commerce, business services, education, health, recreation or tourism – has a different profile, different needs and, in many cases, a different government body. These differences are reflected in its digital spatiality. The urban system is highly fragmented in terms of operation and governance, and this fragmentation is exacerbated by a sea of digital applications for cities and an unlimited number of virtual spaces. The diversity of solutions and software suitable for different districts of a city creates an 'inflationary universe' of digital applications with questionable capacity to enhance the intelligence of cities and its problem-solving capacity. On the contrary, the widespread adoption of intelligent city strategies requires some standardization and simplification, clear solutions that the public administration can choose from a portfolio of solutions that offer documented benefits.

As a counterpoise to the above observations of inflation in terms of applications and strategies of intelligent cities, this article aims to describe some fundamental mechanisms of spatial intelligence that can be implemented in cities and their different districts. In previous publications we have argued that the intelligence of cities is based on a series of knowledge functions that are collectively created and deployed, such as network-based information intelligence and forecasting, technology learning and acquisition, collaborative innovation, product and service promotion, and dissemination (Komninos, 2008, 2009). This article extends these arguments by showing how different cognitive capabilities are activated within different urban arrangements. We argue that despite the great diversity of strategies and applications for intelligent cities, the spatial intelligence of cities relies on a few knowledge generation trajectories. This argument is sustained by the study of multiple cases over the last few years, and especially by insights gained from the study on Bletchley Park and the survey on Cyberport Hong Kong and Smart Amsterdam discussed here. Socio-technological experiments in these communities represent important efforts to create intelligent/smart cities and contribute to a better understanding of the many faces of spatial intelligence. At Bletchley Park large-scale, organized cooperation took place during World War II involving creative people, collective working procedures, rule-based thinking and intelligent machines; in Cyberport Hong Kong we find a set of urban infrastructures that continually improve the skills and talents of the Hong Kong younger population; and in Amsterdam Smart City we find smart systems for collecting and disseminating information in real time that enable citizens to take informed decisions and improve the environmental sustainability of the different city districts.

This article is structured as follows. The next section discusses the concept of spatial intelligence of cities and how the literatures on cyber, digital, intelligent and smart cities have shaped the landscape of intelligent cities. The further three sections describe three different trajectories and architectures of spatial intelligence (orchestration, amplification, instrumentation) that can be found within cities. Each type of spatial intelligence is presented with respect to the case study on Bletchley Park, Cyberport Hong Kong and Smart Amsterdam. Finally, the last section is focused on contemporary challenges of spatial intelligence and the need to balance the development of applications with the integration of digital, institutional and physical space of cities.

SPATIAL INTELLIGENCE OF CITIES

The concept of spatial intelligence refers to the ability of a community to use its intellectual capital, institutions and material infrastructure to deal with a range of problems and challenges. Spatial intelligence emerges from the agglomeration and integration of three types of intelligence: the inventiveness, creativity and intellectual capital of the city's population; the collective intelligence of the city's institutions and social capital; and the artificial intelligence of public and city-wide smart infrastructure, virtual environments and intelligent agents (Komninos, 2008, pp.122–123). Using this spatially combined intellectual capacity, cities can respond effectively to changing socio-economic conditions, address challenges, plan their future, and sustain the prosperity and well-being of citizens.

Intelligent and smart cities constitute a major breakthrough in contemporary urban development and planning literature, which spans over a period of 20 years. The first academic paper on intelligent cities appeared in 1992 (Laterasse, 1992), while the first academic paper on smart cities was also published the same year (Gibson et al., 1992). Since then, these ideas have spread widely, in both theory and practice, and these literatures profoundly changed the dominant discussion of the 1980s and 1990s about cities, post-Fordism, production flexibility, technopoles, social polarization and conflict. The new set of ideas offers a more optimistic perspective for cities: linking their development to the knowledge and innovation economy and the information society.

Two major driving forces sustained the paradigm shift towards intelligent cities. On the one hand, the rising knowledge and innovation economy that sustains contemporary economic development worldwide, and on the other hand, the spread of the Internet and the web as major technological innovations of our era. The urban paradigm of intelligent cities brings these two trajectories together. Urban development has become dependent on innovation ecosystems, knowledge-driven localities, innovation clusters and creative hubs, in which R&D, knowledge, innovation, people's creativity, learning and training are connected by forces of agglomeration and locality, trust, knowledge spillovers and tacit knowledge transmission. In parallel, a new digital spatiality has been added to the physical and institutional space of cities, the agglomeration of city activities, infrastructures, regulation and planning. It is composed of broadband networks, user interfaces, Internet applications, e-services, creating an umbrella of digital communication and cooperation that is situated over the cities. The rise of information communication technologies (ICTs), the Internet and the web alone would not have had a strong impact on cities if contemporary urban agglomerations had not rooted their development in knowledge and innovation.

Digital spatiality constitutes a condition that is historically new for cities as the spaces of agglomeration (population gatherings, geography of economic activities, physical space and infrastructures) and institutional regulation (urban policy, planning, government) have now been enriched by a third digital space. It should be stressed that the new digital spatiality has joined the spatialities of agglomeration and regulation in multiple ways, from enhancing communication, city representation, virtualization of infrastructures, changing activities, optimization of city functions, to the gathering and dissemination of intelligence. These different roles of digital and the different forms of integration between physical, institutional and digital spaces have given birth to a series of concepts within the same event horizon, namely the discussion about cyber, digital, intelligent and smart cities.

Cybercities and cyberspace refer to any type of virtual space generated by a collection of data within the Internet (Shiode, 1997), but the concept also contains the sense of inspection and control with communication and information feedback as preconditions of effective action. Cybercities are primarily either the early wave of e-government applications for city management or more recent technologies for security and control over the urban space, and in some cases the transfer of military methods of tracking, identification and targeting into the governance of urban civil society (Graham, 2010). In a broader sense, a cybercity is conceived as a web-based city formation in which people interact with each other and use services or buy products. However, the 'cyber' prefix refers to a more or less dark side of the virtual space, the 'cyberterrorism' and 'cyborg' dimensions (Antirroiko, 2005).

The digital city literature on the other hand, and the extensive work of Ishida and Isbister (2000), Hiramatsu and Ishida (2001), and Van den Besselaar and Koizumi (2005), is more oriented towards the representation of the city, in early forms via portal-type, panoramic and 3D representations of cities, and later with augmented reality technologies, and urban tagging with RFID (radio frequency identification). Digital cities are connected communities that combine 'broadband communications infrastructure; a flexible, service-oriented computing infrastructure based on open industry standards; and, innovative services to meet the needs of governments and their employees, citizens and businesses' (Yovanof and Hazapis, 2009). The digital city offers a metaphor of the city: an understanding of the physical city through its virtual representation (Ishida, 2000, 2002). However, this literature seems less concerned with the connection between the physical and digital dimensions of cities.

Intelligence comes into the scene with the understanding that digital spaces can improve urban ecosystems, because of their capacity to process information, and sustain learning, innovation and problem-solving within a community. Intelligent cities emerge at the crossing between the knowledge-based development of cities (knowledge cities) and the digital cities of social media. The intelligence of cities, which is attributed to

integration, 'resides in the increasingly effective combination of digital telecommunication networks (the nerves), ubiquitously embedded intelligence (the brains), sensors and tags (the sensory organs), and software (the knowledge and cognitive competence)' (Mitchel, 2007). City intelligence also comes from partnerships and social capital in organizing the development of technologies, skills and learning, and engaging citizens to become involved in creative community participation (Deakin and Allwinkle, 2007). The spatial intelligence of cities is based on a combination of the creative capabilities of the population, knowledge-sharing institutions, and digital applications organizing collective intelligence, which altogether produce a higher ability to innovate that is collaboratively created within the city. From this perspective, an intelligent city is a multi-player territorial innovation system combining knowledge-intensive activities, institutions for cooperation in learning and innovation, and digital communication infrastructure and e-services that increase the problem-solving capabilities of the urban population individually and as a whole (Komninos, 2006).

The recent turn and interest towards smart cities highlights two new concerns: on the one hand the pursuit of sustainability, the desire that a smart city should support a more inclusive, diverse and sustainable urban environment, green cities with less energy consumption and CO_2 emissions (Caragliu et al., 2009; Eurocities, 2009), and on the other hand, the rise of new Internet technologies promoting real world user interfaces with mobile phones, smart devices, sensors, RFID, the semantic web and the Internet-of-Things. Smart city literature focuses on the latest advancements in mobile and pervasive computing, wireless networks, middleware and agent technologies as they become embedded into the physical spaces of cities and are fed continuously with data all around the clock. Smart city applications – with the help of instrumentation and interconnection of mobile devices and sensors that collect and analyse real-world data – improve the ability to forecast and manage urban flows and push city intelligence forward (Chen-Ritzo et al. 2009).

All these developments have created a new landscape of intelligent/smart cities in which collective intelligence, innovation, problem-solving, and the use of smart devices and networks offer advanced city functionality and improved operations. The landscape of intelligent cities is extremely complex and open to creative thinking and new solutions. This is due to the character of digital spatiality that offers limitless alternative solutions and potential spaces. Table 1 gives just an overview of this complexity. Cities are adapting slowly to the new landscape: understanding the possibilities offered by advances in information technologies and organizational settings, developing digital applications and e-services, leveraging new business models, and adapting their innovation and inclusion strategies to smart networks, social media, mobile devices and collaborative solutions.

Critical questions within this large landscape of practices and transformations concern the sources of the spatial intelligence of cities: the structures, mechanisms and architectures that sustain the advanced problem-solving capability of cities. What makes a city intelligent or smart? Which type of spatial intelligence is activated within each district/ sector of the city? Is it a spatial intelligence common to all districts or are different structuring forms activated within different city districts depending on their functional characteristics (manufacturing, commerce, education, recreation) and governance?

The case studies we present in the next three sections show that spatial intelligence of cities follows many different trajectories and takes many different forms. The variable geometries of digital, cyber, smart and intelligent cities and the large number of digital applications actualize many mechanisms that both give structure to and sustain city intelligence. Three forms analysed here are *orchestration*

intelligence, which is based on collaboration and distributed problem-solving within a community; *amplification intelligence*, which is based on people's up-skilling provided by experimental facilities, open platforms and city infrastructure; and *instrumentation intelligence*, based on real-time information, comparative (collective) data analysis and predictive models for better decision-making across city districts. These trajectories of spatial intelligence can work in isolation or in coordination. They provide different levels of problem-solving capability, but they always rely on the connection between the physical, institutional and digital space of cities.

ORCHESTRATION INTELLIGENCE: BLETCHLEY PARK AND THE FIRST INTELLIGENT COMMUNITY

From the moment they began to emerge, cities were embedded with advantages created by spatial proximity such as collaboration, use of common infrastructure, face-to-face communication and the development of trust. The spatial agglomeration of people, activities, buildings and infrastructure was made possible by advances in the division of labour and exchange of goods, and in turn generated a series of positive social and economic effects. Soja (2003), writing about the first urban settlements and cities, insists on 'putting cities first', attributing to synekism – the physical agglomeration of people with a form of political coordination – the capacity to advance creativity, innovation, territorial identity and societal development, that arise from living in dense and heterogeneous agglomerations. Soja refers extensively to *The Economies of Cities* by Jane Jacobs (1969) and the findings in Catal Huyuk, the largest and most developed early city in southern Anatolia, where Jacobs located major innovations and transformations from hunting and gathering to agriculture, the first metallurgy, weaving and crude pottery, which took place because of the existence of the city. These innovations, he argues, as well as every major innovation in

TABLE 1 Intelligent cities landscape

	Genesis	Concept	Architecture	Measurement/performance

Concept and structure	● *Innovation economy of cities*: ecosystems of innovation, global innovation networks, user-driven innovation, cities as Living Labs
	
	● *A digital space over* the urban agglomeration and urban planning/governance
		● *Digital cities*: virtual representation of cities
		● *Cyber cities*: governance/control
		● *Smart cities*: sensors/smart devices/iPhones
		● *Intelligent cities*:
		  ● Intelligent innovation ecosystems
		  ● Web-based collective intelligence
		  ● Agglomeration/integration of human, collective and artificial intelligence
			Layer 1: PHYSICAL SPACE, agglomeration, clusters, people (human intelligence)
			Layer 2: INSTITUTIONAL SPACE, governance, innovation system (collective intelligence)
			Layer 3: DIGITAL SPACE, virtual/smart environments, e-learning, web-based collaboration (artificial intelligence)
				1 Population, education, skills
				2 Knowledge development, innovation institutions, social capital
				3 Broadband networks, smart environments, e-services
				4 Innovation performance, problem-solving capacity, wealth of cities

	Cases: intelligent/smart cities	**Strategies**	**Business models -sustainability**	**Impact**
Strategy	● *ASIA*: Singapore iN15, Taipei, Cyberport, Seoul –Gagnam, Media city, Malaysia MSC Songdo ● *USA*: Florida, Cleveland, Waterloo ● *EU*: Manchester, Glasgow, Issy, Tallin, Stockholm, Helsinki, Amsterdam	● Sector-based strategies ● Cluster or district-based strategies ● Multiple cores and sectors ● Multiple architectures of physical–virtual spaces integration and spatial intelligence	● Public funding, national, EU, other ● Revenue generating opportunities ● Fee-based services ● PPP: public private partnerships ● Valorization of public infrastructure	1 More innovative cities: Global innovation chains, crowd-based innovation, more competitive cities 2 Infrastructure cost reduction: e-services for traffic, energy, water, environment, safety 3 Good governance of cities

Innovation ecosystems	**Types of ecosystems** ● Clusters and districts ● Regional systems/triple helix ● Global and interactive systems ● People-driven innovation ecosystems ● Living Labs	**Innovation platforms** ● Crowdsourcing platforms/ iPhone cities ● Global supply chains ● Academic R&D based platforms ● Technology-based platforms ● Open platforms	**Innovation processes** ● R&D/technology based ● Foresight, forecasting, futures ● Learning curve upgrade ● University–industry cooperation ● Co-design/people-driven innovation ● VC/early-stage funding/spin-offs	**Building blocks of ecosystems** 1 Information collection, processing 2 Technology learning, technology transfer, technology acquisition 3 Collaborative innovation, distributed new product development 4 Innovation promotion, marketing
Web technology	**Intelligence** ● OLAP/Business intelligence ● Data mining ● Benchmarking ● Collective intelligence ● Linked data – Ontologies	**Content management systems** ● Joomla ● Word press ● Wikis ● Mashups ● Semantic web	**Collaboration web** ● Co-design tools ● Online collaboration ● Web 2.0 New product development ● Crowdsourcing platforms	**Visualization** ● Web design, Java, Flash ● Panoramics, Street view ● Google 3D cities ● 3D Studio ● Tagwhat – Augmented reality
Applications and e-services	**Domain 1: city districts/sectors** (1) Manufacturing clusters (2) Commercial areas/CBD (3) Tourism areas/historic centre (4) Incubators/technology parks (5) Universities (6) Port/airport clusters OR in different sectors of the urban economy: industry, services, education, tourism	**Domain 2: city utilities** (1) Mobility and transport (2) Energy management and saving (3) Water and related utilities (4) Broadband, wired and wireless (5) Public spaces of cities	**Domain 3: quality of life** (1) Quality of life services to citizens (2) Health (3) Social care (4) Environmental monitoring/alert (5) Safety in the public space	**Domain 4: city governance** (1) Decision-making/democracy (2) Planning/city governance (3) Administration services to citizens (4) Monitoring, measurement and benchmarking

human society come from cooperation, synergy and multiple savings obtained from living in dense urban settlements. These creative externalities of cities – various types of agglomeration economies, external, scale, scope, location, urbanization – stem, on the one hand, from savings in energy, time and materials, and on the other hand, from collaboration and the creation of synergies. The spatial agglomeration of people and activities produces both savings and synergy. New industrial geography has explained how proximity generates additional externalities in the innovation economy because of informal collaboration, untraded interdependences, knowledge spillovers, trust and transmission of tacit knowledge.

With the digital spatiality extended over cities, collaboration and synergies are scaling up. As citizens come into the digital space, they share more and share it quicker. Interaction becomes easier and synergy stronger. The holy triad of synergy – proximity, trust, communication – is strengthened: proximity increases because the 'other' is just a few clicks away; trust deepens because digital interaction leaves traces; communication intensifies because we have more means and tools for interaction. The sheer scalability of digital interaction and synergy is impressive: scalability being the property of a system that ensures its ability to become enlarged in an elegant manner. Digital interaction enables larger collaboration, more extended supply chains and more end-user participation. Multiple digital technologies enhance the scalability of collaboration, such as co-design tools, collaborative work environments, real-time communication without cost, crowdsourcing solutions, content mash-ups and data interoperability over urban operational systems.

As computers, devices and information systems become embedded into cities, the collaboration patterns among citizens change substantially. Change does not concern scalability only, but the architectures of cooperation as well. New networking architectures emerge, involving both humans and machines. As digital technology transfers tasks from humans to machines, workflows are revised, more tasks are performed by cooperation, machines inspect the follow-up of collaboration patterns, and storing capacity skyrockets. Multiple new solutions of collaboration become possible. For instance, the physico-digital urban system can integrate crowdsourcing and solutions provided by the population, such as content creation, customers improving a product, and a community deciding about a city plan; the urban system can improve individual practices taking into account real-time information and other people's practices; and the system can lower operation costs by more effectively sharing resources and infrastructure. The city ends up with higher problem-solving capability, quicker responses, better quality procedures and lower operation costs: in other words, with higher intelligence. This happens because machine intelligence is added to the human intelligence of citizens and to the collective intelligence of their community.

The first community that successfully practised this form of large-scale cooperation and integration of individual, collective and machine intelligence was Bletchley Park in the UK. The story of Bletchley Park is well known in the World War II code-breaking literature. However, it was never referred to as an intelligent city or intelligent community.

Bletchley Park is located 80 km north-west of London. Bletchley is an ordinary town, a regional urban centre in the county of Buckinghamshire, at the intersection of London and North-Western Railway with a line linking Oxford to Cambridge. Just off the junction, within walking distance from the station, lies Bletchley Park, an estate of about 100 ha with a grand Victorian mansion at the centre of the estate.

The development of Bletchley Park started in August 1939 when the *Government Code and Cypher School* moved from London to Bletchley Park to carry out their code-breaking work in a safer environment. A small group of people was initially settled at Bletchley composed of code-breaking experts, cryptanalytic personnel and university professors from the exact sciences and mathematics. Alan Turing arrived at Bletchley Park in 1939 together with other professors from Cambridge to help set up the methods of analysis and workflow. The work was done in wooden huts, designated by numbers, and brick-built blocks that were constructed after 1939 to house the different sectors of cryptanalysis. In the years thereafter, the personnel of Bletchley Park increased in number at a spectacular rate and by the end of the war they numbered about ten thousand. People came from all fighting services, and were seconded to Bletchley Park because of their skills, and included civilians, authors, diplomats, bankers, journalists and teachers, and many women who received training in routine information processing tasks.

The mission of Bletchley Park was to find the daily settings of the Enigma machines used by the German Army to encode all transmitted messages between the army headquarters, divisions, warships, submarines, port and railway stations, military installations and other installations, and then decode all these messages. It is estimated that by 1942 the German Army had at least a hundred thousand Enigma machines, which produced an enormous traffic of codified messages of vital importance for the daily operation of all army units. The Enigma machine was an electro-mechanical device for encryption and decryption of messages based on polyalphabetic substitution. It relied on interchangeable rotors of 26 letters, initially three and later five, moving rings and a plugboard that permitted variable electrical wiring connecting letters in pairs. Every key press on the keyboard caused one step on the first rotor – after a full rotation the other rotors also moved – and then electrical connections were made that changed the substitution

alphabet used for encryption. Decoding was symmetrical. The receiver had to settle the machine in its initial setting of rotors, rings and plugging, type the coded message and recover the original. The combination of rotor order, the initial position of rotors and plug settings created a very large number of possible configurations. For each setting of rotors there were a trillion ways to connect 10 pairs of letters on the plugboard. It was practically impossible to break the encryption by hand.

The amount of collaborative knowledge work carried out at Bletchley Park was enormous. The park was an 'industry' for information collection, processing, decoding and distribution. About 2,000–6,000 messages were processed and translated daily, while overall 200,000–500,000 German messages were decoded between 1940 and 1945. The impact was also extremely high. The strategic role of Bletchley Park was in the battle for supplies, defeating the U-boats in the Atlantic and securing the inflow of materials, foods and ammunition to Britain. By the end of 1941 the British announced that the problem of maritime supplies had been solved. Historians estimate that the work done in Bletchley Park shortened the war by 2–4 years and saved millions of lives. The philosopher George Steiner described Bletchley Park as the greatest achievement of Britain during the war and perhaps during the whole 20th century.

The work done at Bletchley Park in breaking German communications codes was based on a collaborative workflow between scientists, experts, trained workers and machines that offered increased intelligence to deal with this challenge. The system had all the four essential characteristics that we now attribute to intelligent cities: (1) a creative population working in information and knowledge-intensive activities; (2) institutions and routines for collaboration in knowledge creation and sharing; (3) technological infrastructure for communication, data processing and information analysis; and (4) a proven ability to innovate and solve problems that appear for the first time. Bletchley Park was the first intelligent community ever created.

The methodological solutions about how to break the Enigma ciphers were given by a group of British cryptanalysts and mathematicians at Bletchley Park who continued and enriched the methods devised by Polish mathematicians in previous and simpler models of Enigma machines. The wiring structure of the machines and some fundamental design flaws – no letter could ever be encrypted as itself – were exploited. The breaking of the codes was based on human factors and mistakes made by the Germans. Alan Turing and the Cambridge mathematician Gordon Welchman, who also invented the method of perforated sheets, provided the designs for the new machine – the British Bombe – that could break any Enigma cipher based on an accurate assumption of about twenty letters in the message. Alan Turing contributed with several insights in breaking the Enigma, somehow continuing his theoretical work on computable numbers and the universal machine, bringing these ideas into the physical world.

Key to the success of Bletchley Park was collaboration and workflow integrating the whole process. Cryptanalyst worked as a team. They had to analyse all messages of the day to make assumptions out of the basic setting of the rotors. Codebooks found in sunken submarines or captured ships were also very helpful and provided Enigma ground settings and abbreviations. They had to simulate the entire German classification system, mapping and acronyms. Cryptanalysis acquired meaning only through the coordination of different activities across an extended workflow and solving ciphers was only part of it. There was organized division of labour and specialization into different tasks along the process of intercepting the messages, transferring them to Bletchley Park, code breaking, verification and dissemination to recipients of the information. The raw material came from a web of wireless intercept stations around Britain and overseas. Codebreakers based in the huts were supported by teams who turned the deciphered messages into intelligence reports. The letter from Turing, Welchman, Alexander and Milner-Barry to Churchill in October 1941, asking for more resources at Bletchley Park, personnel, night shifts, interception stations, specialized decoders and support to the Bombes, shows this integrated functioning of the community.

When a cryptanalyst developed an assumption about a possible way of breaking the code in a message, he prepared a menu (called a crib – plain text that corresponded to the cipher text) that was sent to be tested on a Bombe machine. This was an electro-mechanical machine used to discover the set of rotors, the settings of the alphabet rings, and the wiring of the plugboard. The machine would check a million permutations, exclude those containing contradictions and finally reveal how the Enigma machine had been set in order to produce this crib. The Bombe would then provide a solution by discounting every incorrect one in turn. The first Bombe was based on Turing's design and was installed at Bletchley Park in 1940. Subsequent Bombes were equipped with Welchman's diagonal board that could substantially decrease the number of possible rotor settings. In 1944 Colossus, the first digital electronic computer, became operational at Bletchley Park. Colossus was designed to break messages coded on Lorenz machines. The Lorenz machine created more complex ciphers using a code in which each letter of the alphabet was represented by a series of five electrical impulses. Obscuring letters were also generated by Lorenz's 12 rotors. The first Colossus arrived at Bletchley Park in December 1943 and in practical terms Bletchley Park used the world's first electronic computer and digital information processing machine.

Bletchley Park was a prototype of an intelligent community, an urban ecosystem in which orchestration among people, workflows based on institutional rules, and intelligent machines produced radical innovations. The military organization in this case and absence of the spontaneous complexity we find in cities should not undervalue the innovativeness of its design and its effectiveness in dealing with extremely complex problems.

AMPLIFICATION INTELLIGENCE: CYBERPORT HONG KONG UP-SKILLING ON EXPERIMENTAL FACILITIES AND CITY INFRASTRUCTURE

There is, however, another route to the spatial intelligence of cities, which leverages the impact of knowledge-intensive infrastructures and districts that are currently shaping the city's built environment.

The spatial structure of knowledge-based and intelligent cities is actually taking the form of 'knowledge ecosystems and districts over smart networks'. This form is partly due to the need for active management of technological infrastructure and innovation systems, and partly to the development of smart urban networks. The literature on the clustering of innovation has explained the causes of spatial agglomeration and the creation of islands of innovation (Simmie, 1998; Morgan, 2004). Many types of clusters – cohesion, industrial districts, innovative milieu, proximity – with different degrees of internal association and input–output interaction (Hart, 2000) and different sizes conglomerate over the city infrastructure. City networks for mobility, energy, water and utilities, on the other hand, are becoming smarter under the pressure of environmental sustainability and the need to save resources. It is estimated that smart infrastructure, smart grids, sensors, wireless meters and actuators might have a higher impact on energy saving and CO_2 reduction than the total positive effect from renewable energy sources.

Metropolitan plans like the 'Melbourne 2030 Plan' and 'Stockholm's Vision 2030' have clearly adopted this strategy of organizing various types of innovation ecosystems and knowledge-intensive districts over advanced infrastructure, including broadband, telecommunications, energy, multimodal transport and logistics to sustain the development of the innovation economy. Melbourne has institutionalized this type of development via 'knowledge precincts', areas surrounding university campuses in which special land use regulations favour the location of activities that link university infrastructure and R&D, offering opportunities for technology diffusion and cross-fertilization between high-tech businesses, academia and public sector facilities (Yigitcanlar et al., 2008).

All innovation ecosystems profit from technology diffusion, knowledge spillovers and knowledge transfer. However, some are pursuing conscious strategies for involving the wider population of the city, not just producers and technologists, and are creating a flow of new skills entailing education and learning on experimental facilities and the use of advanced information and communication infrastructure. In the case of Living Labs, for instance, users are involved in new product development and testing within real urban environments. Participatory innovation processes integrate *co-creation* activities, bringing together technology push and application pull, *exploration* activities engaging user communities in an earlier stage of the co-creation process, *experimentation* activities, implementing the proper level of technological artefacts to experience live scenarios, and *evaluation* of new ideas and innovative concepts as well as related technological artefacts in real-life situations (Pallot, 2009). To date, after four successive waves of expansion, the European Network of Living Labs (ENoLL) has 212 members from the 27 EU Member States and countries outside the EU, such as Switzerland, Canada, the USA, China, Taiwan, Brazil, Mozambique, Senegal and South Africa. These open and user-centric innovation ecosystems operate in many and diverse activity sectors, such as mobile communications, media, agriculture, food industry, health, medicine, e-government services, smart cities, sports, education and social work.

There are also city ecosystems that act as 'innovation universities' or 'intelligent campuses', which use the built environment of the city and experimental facilities to involve citizens in learning and innovation. Large-scale up-skilling strategies thus become possible: thereby improving the creativity, intelligence and inventiveness of the population, and introducing an 'innovation for all' environment, in which every citizen can become a producer of services and innovations.

Cyberport Hong Kong is an innovation ecosystem that has effectively advanced this strategy of up-skilling, using advanced telecommunication infrastructure and multi-media technologies. It is a new knowledge district located on the west side of Aberdeen Country Park on Hong Kong island. The district has been developed as a government project aimed at developing the knowledge economy throughout Hong Kong. As an independent technology district, Cyberport is focusing on professional and enterprise development, offering an open platform for creative ideas to flourish and start-ups to be created in the field of media technologies. The district is wholly owned by the Hong Kong SAR Government and managed by the Cyberport Management Company Limited.

Cyberport includes many different activities and land uses. Within a relatively small piece of land of 24 ha, there is an enterprise zone with four quality buildings that host about 100 information technology and media companies, a research institute, business incubator, conference centre, shopping mall, 5-star hotel – Le Meridien, a huge housing complex and a large park at the heart of Cyberport that also extends along the coastline. The area is served by fibre optic and copper networks offering high-speed broadband connections and a wide range of digital services and laboratory equipment. Buildings in the technology zone are grade-A intelligent office buildings. All these activities

are organized into four different zones: the technology zone with Cyberport 1, 2, 3 and 4 buildings, the commercial zone with the mall and the hotel, the residential zone, and the park and open area zone. Despite this functional division, the relatively small surface of the district and the openness here create a continuum of uses as all the spaces are accessible to the community of the district.

Activities and land uses have been selected to promote the mission of the district and ensure its sustainability. Cyberport was developed on public land and the construction work took place from 2000 to 2008. The funding scheme foresaw a split into two parts: the Cyberport zone and the ancillary residential zone. The mission of the Cyberport zone was to create a strategic cluster of leading information technology and information services companies and a critical mass of professionals in these sectors. The mission of the residential zone was to generate revenue for the Cyberport project. A development company acquired part of the land (about 20 per cent of the plot) together with the infrastructure already on-site to build the residential zone. The developer (Cyber-Port Limited) was responsible for the total construction costs of both Cyberport and the housing complex (Hong King Legislative Council, 2002). The residential zone includes eight 50-storey-high buildings and two lower complexes – two to five storeys – for high-income residences along the coast. Overall, 2800 homes were built. In return for the concession of the land and infrastructure of the residential zone, the developer delivered the technology zone as a turnkey solution, with Cyberport 1, 2, 3 and 4, the shopping mall arcade and the 5-star hotel operated by Le Meridien, and the central park. Revenue generated by the commercial zone – mall and hotel – run in the technology zone and cover training, learning and incubation expenses. The district was publicly funded and serves the public interest. This genuine funding model provided both the development and operation funds for Cyberport 1, 2, 3, 4, and secured the public character of the district.

Cyberport should not be seen as the usual technology district or technology park. It is an ecosystem that nurtures talent in the media industry, turning skills and talent into start-ups. It amplifies the skills and creativities of the Hong Kong population using experimental digital infrastructure and open platforms. The objectives are technology diffusion, up-skilling and the enhancement of human capabilities. Cyberport is a creative community supplied with advanced communication and media infrastructure and digital connectivity. 'Cyberport identifies, nurtures, attracts and sustains talent so it is able to mobilize ideas, talents and creative organisations. It is a creative milieu; a place that contains the necessary requirements in terms of hard and soft infrastructure to generate a flow of ideas and inventions' (Interview with CEO of Cyberport N. Yang). The focus of the district is the information technology (IT) and multimedia sector, where it sustains a creative community. Technologies and applications that have been developed in Hong Kong universities or the Technology Park can be transferred to the younger generation through practical learning and experimental training. Training from the world's leading media and IT companies is provided together with the laboratory equipment and start-up funding for follow-up training that promotes entrepreneurship.

To achieve these objectives, Cyberport has developed state-of-the-art infrastructure, media equipment and digital services that are organized as open technology platforms. Each platform serves a specific objective of training, creativity and entrepreneurship.

The Digital Entertainment Incubation and Training Programme is a platform whose objective is to build and promote entrepreneurship and competence in the digital entertainment industry, focusing on business skills, games, animation and digital entertainment, and to enhance networking with industry, as well as to promote the awareness and interest of the younger generation in digital entertainment.

The Digital Media Centre is a unique state-of-the-art digital multimedia creation facility, whose objective is to offer software and hardware support to content developers, multimedia professionals, and small- and medium-sized enterprises.

The iResource Centre is a digital content storage platform, which serves as a trusted marketplace and clearing house for the aggregation, protection, license issuance and distribution of digital content.

The Testing and Certification of Wireless Communication Platform provides continuous mobile communication services and coverage of mobile phone signals (3G, GSM, CDMA and PCS) in both outdoor and indoor areas within Cyberport in cooperation with major mobile communications service operators.

The Cyberport Institute was established by the University of Hong Kong to introduce and run IT courses for talented people and to support various IT development and related businesses in Hong Kong.

These open technology platforms are operated in cooperation with industry leaders who are the founding industrial partners. Cisco, Hewlett Packard, IBM, Microsoft, Oracle and PCCW have been involved through sponsorship programmes, while the students benefit from access to top-of-the-market technologies, scholarships, placement opportunities and employment.

The dual mechanism described above – open digital technology platforms and real-estate-based sustainability – provides an open-ended mechanism for professional training and up-skilling. The setting enhances human capabilities and intelligence by simultaneously using hard urban infrastructure and soft digital technologies and services. Developed on public land, Cyberport is creating intelligence through skills, human development programmes and a real estate business model, which spreads out into the entire urban system of Hong Kong.

INSTRUMENTATION INTELLIGENCE: AMSTERDAM SMART CITY REAL-TIME DECISION-MAKING ACROSS CITY DISTRICTS

One of the most significant recent contributions to the intelligence of cities debate comes from the initiative developed by IBM 'Smart Planet – Smarter Cities'. IBM proposes a city intelligence solution based on the combination of networks, meters and data modelling. Digital technologies can transform cities and optimize the use of infrastructure and their finite resources, driving efficiency and increased effectiveness, by making city systems (1) interconnected, (2) instrumented and (3) intelligent. *Interconnection* means that different parts of a core system can be joined and communicate with each other, turning data into information. *Instrumentation* of a city's system means that running that system produces data on key performance indicators and the system becomes measurable with instruments and smart meters. *Intelligence* refers to the ability to use the information gathered to model patterns of behaviour, develop predictive models of likely outcomes, allowing better decision-making and informed actions (Dirks and Keeling, 2009; IBM, 2010). It is estimated that this instrumentation intelligence might cut city traffic by as much as 20 per cent, save energy by up to 15 per cent, lower the cost of therapy by as much as 90 per cent and substantially reduce the city's budget spent on public safety (Kaiserswerth, 2010). IBM is testing this concept through partnerships with cities worldwide. In many cities the company and local administrations work together to provide services in energy, water management and transportation, reducing the city's impact on the environment. Pilot testing and experimental facilities provide information on how to consume better electricity, water, natural gas and oil.

The same concept is pursued at research level from the Future Internet Research (FIRE) initiative, the European FP7-ICT programme that is funding the experimental facility of 'Smart Santander' in the city of Santander in northern Spain. The facility will develop a network of 20,000 sensors and devices embedded into the physical space of the city. Many different elements of the city will be instrumented: infrastructures with sensors, actuators, tags and readers; utilities for power, water, gas and waste; buildings and houses; transport infrastructure on roads, rail and interchange points; and mobility elements in vehicles and goods. Devices will connect over a common IP infrastructure using cellular, radio meshed networks and available broadband (Krco, 2010). The facility will be open to researchers, end users and service providers to test architectures and enabling technologies, pilot applications, the interaction and management of protocols, and support services such as discovery, identity management and security, and the social acceptance of services related to the Internet-of-Things (see www.smartsantander.eu/).

Instrumentation intelligence is also widely pursued in Amsterdam Smart City. Smart devices and wireless meters transmit information over broadband networks and provide intelligence that citizens and organizations of the city can use to optimize their practice. Decisions can be made with respect to accurate and on-time information provided by smart devices or by the crowd. Different solutions for this type of logic are being implemented in different districts of the city: housing and living (West Orange, Geuzenveld, Haarlem, 'Onze Energie'), working (ITO Tower, monumental buildings, employee contest), mobility (Ship to Grid, 'Moet je Watt') and public space (Climate Street, smart schools, ZonSpot, smart swimming) (Baron, 2011). In the Haarlem area for example, 250 users can test an energy management system and get insight into the energy consumption of appliances, enabling monitoring of energy usage and appliances to be remotely switched on and off. In the Geuzenveld neighbourhood, 500 homes have been provided with smart meters and energy displays to become aware of energy consumption and discuss energy savings at brainstorming sessions. In the West Orange project, 500 households have been provided with smart meters and displays, and a personal energy saving goal is set for every household. The overall objective is to save at least 14 per cent energy and reduce CO_2 emissions by an equal amount. The ITO tower, a large multi-tenant office building, is testing which smart building technologies, cooperative agreements and practices can make office buildings more sustainable. Information gained by smart plugs and insight based on data analysis will be used to provide more efficient solutions. In the Utrechtsestraat, a shopping street with numerous cafés and restaurants, 140 small enterprises are testing solutions for a more sustainable environment: logistics using electric vehicles, energy-saving lamps for street lighting dimmed during quiet times, solar-powered garbage compacters, smart meters and displays for energy consumption, and incentives and benefits arising from energy savings (Amsterdam Smart City, 2009). The city also recently experimented with crowdsourcing, co-creation and open innovation to involve citizens in finding better solutions for public space and mobility. Ambitious goals were set to reduce CO_2 emissions by 40 and 20 per cent in 2025 from 1990 baseline. Key performance indicators show that these goals can be achieved. In the Climate street, already more than 50 per cent sustainable waste collection and 10 per cent energy saving are recorded.

DISCUSSION

Orchestration, amplification and instrumentation intelligence illustrate different paths of spatial intelligence leading to more efficient cities. These architectures of spatial intelligence are based on different forms of integration among individuals, institutional frameworks of collaboration, computers and embedded systems. Orchestration intelligence relies mainly on integration along community-based workflows; amplification intelligence integrates

skills, digital tools and city infrastructures, using the city as an open platform for creativity; and instrumentation intelligence a integrates city's infrastructure, activity data flows, measurement devices and predictive modelling. Spatial intelligence enabled by agglomeration, collaboration and city infrastructure creates more efficient cities by improving the innovation ecosystems of industry, commerce, services, transport and utilities that operate within cities.

Meanwhile, future Internet and future media research are bringing in new solutions in terms of infrastructure (cloud computing, RFIDs, sensors, real-world user interfaces, mobile devices), data (open data, linked data) and trusted services. Solutions are being engineered in all domains of cities: the *innovation economy* of cities with the different districts, sectors of economic activity and ecosystems that they contain; the *utilities* of cities with their different networks, flows and infrastructure; and the *governance* of cities with services to citizens, decision-making procedures, participation and democracy. At least 20 different domains of cities can be identified as fields of intelligent/smart city applications with thousands of applications. However, the impact of this technological breakthrough on cities is still very limited.

A public consultation on the priorities of European urban and regional policy has identified three major urban and regional objectives for the coming years (European Commission, 2008). Competitiveness should continue to be at the heart of European cohesion policy, sustained by research, innovation and upgrading of skills, which altogether drive towards a knowledge economy. Active labour markets that sustain employment and reduce the risk of poverty are also a high priority; to a large degree poverty is a consequence of job losses. The third objective is environmental sustainability: coupled with the need to save energy, use alternative energy sources, ensure lower CO_2 emissions, reduce the carbon footprint of cities and buildings, and sustain living ecosystems.

Smart or intelligent cities are expected to contribute to these challenges and provide sound solutions. However, to date most smart/intelligent city solutions have had limited impact on the challenges of competitiveness, employment and sustainability of cities. This mismatch signifies several things: either smart cities are not well targeted on city challenges, solutions are more technology push than demand driven, or cities have not efficiently implemented spatial intelligence. All explanations hold, and cities with all the technology and institutions they actually have are not yet sufficiently intelligent. Even applications that are considered very successful, such as Groupon, SeeClickFix and smart phones CityTourApps, do not change cities in a radical way. By and large, contemporary solutions are lagging in terms of the level of achievement and social impact reached by Bletchley Park.

The contradiction is that all the number of applications for digital, cyber, smart and intelligent cities has so far had limited actual impact on and been of limited effectiveness in terms of the major challenges facing cities. The reason is that we still lack a deeper understanding about what makes a city intelligent. To date, digital applications for cities are technology rather than demand and needs driven and bear little connection to the challenges of cities in the fields of the city's competitiveness, utilities and governance. This mismatch limits their impact and prevents the integration of digital spaces into the development processes and welfare of cities. We are still in the age of digital rather than smart or intelligent cities. All definitions of intelligent/smart cities stress the use of ICTs to make cities more innovative and efficient. But they do not stress the need for integration among innovation actors, open connected communities, digital applications, monitoring and measurement, which altogether sustain city intelligence.

At this level we should search for creative solutions, living labs to experiment with architectures that bring all these communities closer, and integrate urban workflows, innovation processes and IT applications. Consequently, research should focus more on architectures of integration between the digital and physical aspects of cities. The need for creative solutions entailing overall architectures linking the physical, institutional and digital space of cities is much greater than the need for stand-alone applications and technological solutions. We have to engineer integrated solutions for every sector, district and innovation ecosystem of a city, as integration is the key to higher spatial intelligence.

REFERENCES

Amsterdam Smart City, 2009, *Introduction Amsterdam Smart City*, Municipality of Amsterdam. [available at http://amster damsmartcity.com/assets/media/factsheet_launch_Amsterdam_ Smart_City_June_3rd.pdf].

Antirroiko, A.V., 2005, *Cybercity, Encyclopedia of the City*, Routledge, London.

Baron, G., 2011, 'Amsterdam Smart City', Amsterdam Innovation Motor, unpublished paper.

Caragliu, A., Del Bo, C., Nijkamp, P., 2009, 'Smart cities in Europe', Research Memoranda 0048, VU University Amsterdam, Faculty of Economics, Business Administration and Econometrics.

Chen-Ritzo, C.H., Harrison, C., Paraszczak, J., Parr, F., 2009, 'Instrumenting the planet', *IBM Journal of Research and Development* 53(3), 338–353.

Deakin, M., Allwinkle, S., 2007, 'Urban regeneration and sustainable communities: the role networks, innovation and creativity in building successful partnerships', *Journal of Urban Technology* 14(1), 77–91.

Dirks, S., Keeling, M., 2009, *A Vision of Smarter Cities*, Centre for Economic Development, Dublin, Ireland.

Eurocities, 2009, *Smart Cities*, workshop report, 16–17 November 2010, Brussels.

European Commission, 2008, *Growing Regions, Growing Europe*, Fifth progress report on economic and social cohesion, European Commission COM(2008) 371 final.

Gibson, D.V., Kozmetsky, G., Smilor, R.W. (eds), 1992, *The Technopolis Phenomenon: Smart Cities, Fast Systems, Global Networks*, Rowman and Littlefield, New York.

Graham, S., 2010, *Cities Under Siege: The New Military Urbanism*, Verso Books, London.

Hart, D.A., 2000, *Innovation Clusters: Key concepts*, Working paper, Department of Land Management and Development, and School of Planning Studies, The University of Reading, United Kingdom.

Hiramatsu, K., Ishida, T., 2001, 'An augmented web space for digital cities', Symposium on Applications and the Internet Proceedings [available at http://ieeexplore.ieee.org/xpl/freeabs_all.jsp?arnumber=905173].

Hollands, R.G., 2008, 'Will the real smart city please stand up? Creative, progressive or just entrepreneurial', *City* **12**(3), 303–320.

Hong King Legislative Council, 2002, 'Background brief on Cyberport', Legislative Council Secretariat [available at www.legco.gov.hk/yr01-02/english/panels/itb/papers/itb0708cb1-2172-1e.pdf].

IBM, 2010, *A Vision of Smarter Cities: How Cities Can Lead the Way into a Prosperous and Sustainable Future*, IBM Global Services.

Ishida, T., 2000, 'Understanding digital cities', in T. Ishida, K. Isbister (eds), *Digital Cities: Experiences, Technologies and Future Perspectives*, Lectures Notes in Computer Science, Vol. 1765, Springer-Verlag, Heidelberg, 7–17.

Ishida, T., 2002, 'Digital city Kyoto', *Communications of the ACM* **45**(7), 76–81.

Ishida, T., Isbister, K. (eds), 2000, *Digital Cities: Technologies, Experiences, and Future Perspectives*, Springer-Verlag, Berlin.

Jacobs, J., 1969, *The Economy of Cities*, Random House, New York.

Kaiserswerth, M., 2010, *Creating a Smarter Planet: One Collaboration at a Time*, IBM Research Zurich [available at www.earto.eu/fileadmin/content/01_Seminars___Conferences/AC_2010/4-Matthias_Kaiserswerth.pdf].

Komninos, N., 2006, 'The architecture of intelligent cities', Intelligent Environments 06 Proceedings, Institution of Engineering and Technology, 13–20.

Komninos, N., 2008, *Intelligent Cities and Globalisation of Innovation Networks*, Routledge, London and New York.

Komninos, N., 2009, 'Intelligent cities: towards interactive and global innovation environments', *International Journal of Innovation and Regional Development* **1**(4), 337–355.

Krco, S., 2010, *SmartSantander – A Smart City Example*, ICT event 2010, 27–29 September, Brussels, Belgium.

Laterasse, J., 1992, 'The intelligent city', in F. Rowe, P. Veltz (eds), *Telecom, Companies, Territories*, Presses de L'ENPC, Paris.

Mitchell, W., 2007, 'Intelligent cities', e-Journal on the Knowledge Society. [available at www.uoc.edu/uocpapers/eng].

Morgan, K., 2004, 'The exaggerated death of geography: learning, proximity and territorial innovation systems', *Journal of Economic Geography* **4**(1), 3–21.

Pallot, M., 2009, 'Engaging Users into Research and Innovation: The Living Lab Approach as a user centred open innovation ecosystem' [available at www.cwe-projects.eu/bscw/bscw.cgi/1760838?id=715404_1760838].

Shiode, N., 1997, 'An outlook for urban planning in cyberspace: toward the construction of cyber cities with the application of unique characteristics of cyberspace', Online Planning Journal, Centre for Advanced Spatial Analysis, University College London [available at www.casa.ucl.ac.uk/planning/articles2/olp.htm].

Simmie, J.M., 1998, 'Reasons for the development of "Islands of innovation". Evidence from Hertfordshire', *Urban Studies* **35**(8), 1261–1289.

Soja, E., 2003, 'Writing the city spatially', *City* **7**(3), 269–280.

URENIO, 2008, *Intelligent Thessaloniki: Design of a Pilot Project of Innovation and Entrepreneurship*, Report to the Ministry of Development [available at www.urenio.org/2009/01/02/intelligent-thessaloniki].

Van den Besselaar, P., Koizumi, S., 2005, *Digital Cities III. Information Technologies for Social Capital: Cross-cultural Perspectives*, Third International Digital Cities Workshop, Amsterdam, Springer-Verlag, Berlin.

Yigitcanlar, T., O'Connor, K., Westerman, C., 2008, 'The making of knowledge cities: Melbourne's knowledge-based urban development experience', *Cities* **25**(2), 63–72.

Yovanof, G.S., Hazapis, G.N., 2009, 'An architectural framework and enabling wireless technologies for digital cities & intelligent urban environments', *Wireless Personal Communications* **49**(3), 445–463.

The embedded intelligence of smart cities

Mark Deakin

Edinburgh Napier University, Edinburgh, UK

This article offers an extensive review of Mitchell's thesis on the transition from the city of bits to e-topia and finds it wanting. It suggests that the problems encountered with the thesis lie with the lack of substantive insight it offers into the embedded intelligence of smart cities. Although problematic in itself, the article also suggests that if the difficulties experienced were only methodological they might perhaps be manageable, but the problem is that they run deeper than this and relate to more substantive issues that surround the trajectory of the thesis. This is a critical insight of some significance because if the trajectory of e-topia is not in the direction of either the embedded intelligence of smart cities, or the information and communication technologies of digitally inclusive regeneration platforms, then the question arises as to whether the thesis can be a progressive force for change, or merely a way of reproducing the status quo.

INTRODUCTION

Mitchell's (1995) book on the *City of Bits* sets out a vision of urban life literally done to bits, left fragmented and in danger of coming unstuck. Mitchell's (1999) next book on e-topia provides the counter-point to this vision of urban life and a scenario where the city is no longer left in bits and pieces, but a place where it all comes together. As Mitchell (2004) states in his more recent book: *Me ++: the Cyborg-Self and the Networked City*, all this 'coming together' is possible because: 'the trial separation of bits and atoms is now over' and this 'post-AD 2000 dissolution of the boundaries between the virtual and physical' is what makes everything worth playing for (p.3). Worth playing for because this 'coming together' of the virtual and physical is something that not only needs to

be networked, but embedded in the intelligence which architects, planners, engineers and surveyors require to make cities smart (Mitchell, 2004).

Although this thesis on the 'coming together' of the virtual and physical and dissolution of the boundaries between 'cyber and meat space' is compelling, it has to be recognized that there are a number of concerns surrounding the technical, environmental and social status of the embedded intelligence currently available for planners, architects, engineers and surveyors to make cities smart.

CONCERNS WITH THE STATUS OF MITCHELL'S THESIS

The first rests with the ability of the thesis to cope with what Mitchell refers to as: 'ancient concerns' surrounding the ecology and equity of urban development and sustainability of the lean, mean and green strategy advanced to explain information society's process of dematerialization (what he refers to as the shedding of atoms). Here the concern is not so much with the utopian legacy of such a vision, but the tendency the thesis has to 'repeat the mistakes of the past' by failing to acknowledge that techno-topian solutions of this kind leaves cities without the means by which to deal with the ecology and equity of development. For the likes of Graham and Marvin (1996, 2001), any such absence of means is seen as leaving the thesis open to the accusation of being yet another kind of environmental determinism, albeit on this occasion one with a particularly keen interest in the networks assembled to embed the intelligence of smart cities.

Mitchell's response to such accusations is tactical and astute, because while clearly locked into the environmental determinism of the techno-topian legacy drawn attention to by Graham and Marvin, the thesis manages to side-step this issue. Moreover, it manages to do this by asserting that the late–modern experience of urban life shall be neither utopian, nor dystopian, but e-topian. Although a clever tactic, in the sense that Mitchell's response clearly leaves the technological underpinnings of the thesis intact, this tends to represent e-topia as a thesis literally on the run, not burdened by the dead weight of the past, but light and agile enough to keep moving forward.

The way the thesis proposes to achieve this is instructive and reveals a lot about its ultimate objective. This is because while e-topia is seen to mark a break with the past, dis-embedding in situ practices, 'churning' everything up and turning things around, all that follows in its wake is perceived as being integrated back into the increasingly carbon-based and silicate-permeated body of urban life which such developments pave the way for. That body of urban life, which is now seen to

provide cities with the platforms (computational frameworks, hardware, software, operational systems and programmes of coded languages), architects, planners, engineers and surveyors, need to be smart in resizing communities and building the recombinant spaces also required to reconcile everything wrapped up in the displacement and re-location this late–modern process of globalization produces.

WHAT THE EMERGING CRITIQUE REVEALS

Although the thesis may stress all the dis-embedding, churn, displacement and re-location wrapped up in the process of globalization is virtuous, not least because it offers the possibility of resizing communities as recombinant spaces which are reconciliatory, unfortunately it neither has the foundation nor superstructure to give this claim any more substance than the force of words used to advance it. For all the thesis has is the idea of putting an end to the trial separation of bits and atoms and call from the professional community of architects, planners and engineers to respond in a way never before thought possible. The problem with this lies with the tendency this well-narrated, deeply thought-out and heart-warming thesis has to shout hard and loud about the need for such a response, but remain silent on the methodology required. That is, remain silent on how the aforementioned professions can embed the intelligence needed for cities to be smart in resizing the communities required for their recombination to be reconciliatory.

These concerns are noticeable for the fact they tend to bring Mitchell's representation of e-topia as urban life where it all comes together into question and cast doubt on the vision of the future the thesis sets out. What the emerging critique reveals is that: if 'information society' is to fully grasp the opportunity e-topia offers to be reconciliatory, we first of all need to lose its environmental determinism, and secondly, see whether the techno-topian legacy which the thesis harbours is only loosely linked to the embedded intelligence of smart cities.

To decouple the determinism of the techno-topian legacy from the intelligence of smart cities and thereby retain the opportunity e-topia has to be reconciliatory is a tall order. This is clear from Mitchell's own discussion on the city of bits surfacing in *High Technology in Low Income Communities* (Mitchell, 2001). Here Mitchell draws attention to the champions of this reconciliation – architects like Calthorpe (1993), Katz (1993) and Horan (2000) who are taking the lead and responding in a way never before thought possible. In a way, the likes of Calthorpe, Katz and Horan contend, that allows their particular brand of new urbanism to be reconciliatory in decoupling the determinism of the techno-topian legacy from the embedded intelligence of smart cities.

In many ways though, it is evident what their particular brand of new urbanism offers is little more than a mirror image of what Mitchell's thesis does: that is a means to side-step questions about the embedded intelligence of smart cities. The problem with this tactic lies with the methodological gap it leaves for the professional bodies the thesis is supposed to serve. For in its current state, the thesis leaves them in the unfortunate situation whereby they are unable to offer any critical insight into the embedded intelligence of smart cities, let alone take on the role of intelligent agents able to search out any opportunities there are for cities to be smart.

Although problematic itself, if the difficulties experienced were only methodological they might perhaps be manageable. The problem is that they run deeper than this, and their knock-on effects relate to more substantive issues surrounding the trajectory of Mitchell's thesis. In particular, they relate to whether or not the response from the professional bodies in question is constructive in embedding the intelligence needed to resize communities and build the recombinant spaces required for cities to become smart. Furthermore, they

raise questions as to whether all this resizing of communities and building of recombinant spaces turns on their use of information and communication technologies (ICTs) and if the intelligence this generates is capable of reconciling one with the other.

This is an important point to stress because if the trajectory is not in this direction, then the question of whether or not all this intelligence can be seen as being smart, vis-à-vis a progressive force for change, or merely a way of reproducing the status quo also surfaces. This matter arises because of what Graham and Marvin have referred to as the tendency towards splintering urbanism. According to their thesis, urban life is no longer able to support the sheer weight of material that cities are expected to carry. This is because their scenario has a vision of the future, which is the direct opposite of the reconciliation that Mitchell sets out and that merely ends up being destructive, doing little more than building the capacity which there is for the urban life of cities to be played out in even more dysfunctionally separated communities.

In many ways, this representation of splintering urbanism provides what can only be referred to as the antithesis of Mitchell's e-topia. An antithesis that goes a long way to search out, uncover and expose the other side of the thesis and which does this in an attempt to throw light on the 'futureless' plight of the urban poor as low-income communities living in the deprived quarters of the city. From this account of what is euphemistically referred to as the fragmentation of urban places as electronic spaces, it is evident that the problems with Mitchell's thesis on e-topia are as much substantive as methodological, the former holding the key to unlocking the latter.

The key thing to bear in mind with all of this is that everything, that is, e-topia, or splintering urbanism, hangs on whether or not the embedded intelligence of cities is smart enough to meet the ecological integrity and equity that is required to stop forcing communities apart and support their coming together. So, in this sense Mitchell is right, there is still everything to play for and the risk of the professions not taking action to resize communities as recombinant spaces is too great to contemplate. For if no action is taken, e-topia will remain little more than a speculative vision of urban life, incapable of representing cities as leading examples of what is either intelligent or smart about such developments.

THE CHALLENGE

Accepting this, the question we currently face is not so much about whether to work with the vision e-topia sets out, or abandon it, but how best to meet the criticisms levelled at it. However, in accepting this, we subsequently come up against a challenge of some magnitude. This is because there is not only the question of how to meet the criticisms, but draw a line under them, move on and in effect do what others have as yet been unable to. That is, do nothing less than show how the vision of e-topia is being developed as a means to demonstrate the potential which exists for the embedded intelligence of cities to be smart in allowing the resizing of low-income communities to be constructive and build spaces which are ecologically sound and equitable.

The instruction we get from Mitchell on this matter appears in his statement on the materiality of the e-topia thesis in *Me ++: The Cyborg-Self and the Networked City*. Here Mitchell suggests that it is not virtual versus physical, nor cyber versus meat space that is significant, but the 'networked intelligence being embedded everywhere' in cities, which is the critical factor in them becoming lean, mean green and smart. This is because he suggests that we are increasingly living out our lives in places 'where electronic information flows, mobile bodies and physical spaces interact in engaging ways', with these 'occurrences' in turn pointing the way to the architecture of the twenty-first century.

Yet again, however, what this 'architecture of the twenty-first century' means for the urban life of cities in not clear and highly controversial. Especially, if we contrast this post-2000AD (literally, after dematerialization) account of late–modern globalization with the position taken by Mitchell (2005) in his more recent publication: *Placing Words*. Here all the significance previously lavished on the new subjectivity of the so-called cyborg-self and their civic existence as wireless bi-peds appears to be set aside. Here he suggests the node-based subjectivity of the cyborg-self is perhaps best understood, not so much as the limb-like extension and sensory augmentation of urban life immersed in the programmable code of the city's de-privatized space, but as the context-specific language of social capital.

Unlike Mitchell's declaration about the trial separation of atoms and bits being over, it appears that here in *Placing Words*, their materiality, that is, tangible form and content, is something which is still very much in the process of being brought back together; so what their re-coupling means can be put on trial and understood in the everyday language of urban life as we have come to know it; that is to say, in the atomistic, bitty, fragmented, fragile, anxious and insecure encounters of everyday urban life and which we all share with other members of civil society.

STAKING OUT THE LANDSCAPE

The landscape this article targets, aims to stakeout and occupy, is the middle ground between the 'high-level' issues of the cyborg-self and those found at the 'grass roots' level of everyday linguistic practices (Mitchell's electronic space and Graham and Marvin's urban place, respectively). This is because it is here where 'what it all means' gets 'bottomed out' as part of the emerging discourse on the embedded intelligence of smart cities, represented as basic values (e.g. ecological integrity and equity) underpinning the 'low-level' actions (planning, property development, design and construction activities) supporting their digitally inclusive regeneration (Curwell et al., 2004).

Approaching the matter in this way makes it possible to run vertically, digging deep into the planning and development of cities and use this as the basis to move horizontally. That is, as a basis to be constructive in using ICTs to build a platform of services which are capable of supporting a digitally inclusive regeneration (Cooper et al., 2005).

The outcome of this is a platform of services which have the institutional depth needed for any such multi-scalar resizing to be constructive in building bridges between the spaces that have previously been divided. Those types of bridge-building exercises this article argues are of particular concern to the 'political body' of civil society and the public's call not for what has euphemistically become known as cyber, or meat-space, but for a greater, more extensive and higher level of participation in decisions taken about material basis of urban life. Greater in the sense that such participation is not just limited to urban land-use planning, but extends into the property development, design, construction, operation and use of buildings. More extensive in the sense the participation in question is not limited to the use of urban land, but 'scaled-up' and 'resized', using the step-wise logic of planning, property development, design and construction. That is, 'scaled-up' and 'resized' into a type of 'step-wise' logic which lifts us onto a stage no longer limited to matters of environmental concern, but instead able to reach out, extend beyond, consult with and include deliberations on matters about the social, environmental and economic future of urban life.

TAKING THE EMBEDDED INTELLIGENCE OF SMART CITIES FULL CIRCLE

From this vantage point, it becomes possible to point towards what this all means. This in turn takes the investigation into the embedded intelligence of smart cities *full circle* and

begins to answer the questions posed by the critics of Mitchell's thesis.

These questions will be answered by letting what follows outline urban life as we shall come to know it! That is to say, as a whole new landscape that seeks to sustain the urban life of cities through the planning, property development, design and construction of places, qualified in terms of the ecological integrity and equity of the villages and neighbourhoods making up the multi-scalar resizing of communities. Those multi-scalar and resized communities whose recombinant spaces are no longer alien, but now familiar enough – as villages and neighbourhoods – for the public to participate in constructing because the decisions taken about their design and layout have a bearing on the environmental and social future of their urban life.

The search for a representation of embedded intelligence, which is the antithesis of an environmentally deterministic perspective of urban life and is smart in offering cities a role in 'making a place for low income communities', turns attention away from 'the electronic spaces of urban places' and towards the role of ICTs as (plat)forms of social capital (Halpern, 2005). For in turning attention towards the embedded intelligence of social capital, it subsequently becomes possible to recognize the critical role which the conversations, dialogues and discourses of everyday urban life play in the ability cities have to be smart in creating not only the norms, rules and expectations of the multi-scalar resizing communities are subject to, but the recombinant spaces that are also part of this digitally inclusive regeneration.

This achieves what Mitchell makes clear is needed in his reference to Bretch's (1932) comments on the role of 'the radio as an apparatus of communication' (Mitchell, 2004). In particular, the need for the type of two-way information flow and multi-channelled communication Mitchell believes to be the basis of the collaborative platforms, consensus building, ecological integrity, equity and democratic renewal required to rescale communities and 'size them up' as the recombinant spaces of urban life. This provides what Mitchell refers to as:

a strategy that draws upon the lessons of the internet [which], is to think of [the platform] as a communal resource, like the old village commons, or the land available to the squatter community. [Because this means] anyone can use it as long as they follow a few rules ... (2005, p.56).

The lesson learnt from this being to build such platforms from what Mitchell calls:

The viral propagation of web links and email lists to support grass roots campaigning which are not constrained by distance. Blogs and online forum which substitute highly interactive discussion for the broadcasting of packaged messages (Mitchell, 2005, p.74).

Although this points towards a strategy for the development of a collaborative platform, the lack of focus it offers on either the ICTs, or social capital of such structures, means the statement about building consensus on the multi-scalar resizing of communities and as the recombinant spaces of urban life is only concerned with the city's ecology and not the equity of resource distribution. Questions about equal access to and distribution of the opportunities such platforms offer to secure such services appear to be side-stepped. This is difficult because it means Mitchell's statement on the 'strategic response' tends to give out the wrong message. For while the message conveyed suggests that it is relatively easy to construct such a platform and build the respective user services, experience teaches us that this is anything but the case. Anything but the case for the simple reason the digital divide persists and the ICTs needed to bridge it

are not available on mass for low-income communities to access.

It would appear that if we were to adopt this strategy, the urban poor and dispossessed would remain sidelined and systematically excluded from what Mitchell refers to as the multi-scalar resizing of community and recombination of urban life which is currently being 'played-out' in the villages, neighbourhoods and districts of cities: This in turn producing not only no-go areas, but no-flow environments, without any economic, or social future to boot!

The point made here is that in low-income communities the challenge is even greater because we are starting not just from such a low base-line, but a level of urban development which is also excluded from the mainstream. Excluded from the mainstream for the reason the communities in question do not possess the embedded intelligence needed to be smart. That is, undergo such a multi-scalar resizing in line with the logic of the recombinant spaces which is being imposed upon them as a requirement of this digitally inclusive regeneration.

An instructive account of how a semantic web-based learning platform and knowledge management system capable of networking the types of electronically enhanced service developments outlined here can be used as a platform for digitally inclusive regeneration is reported by Deakin and Allwinkle (2006, 2007) and set out in Deakin (2009a, 2009b).

This platform is drawn from an assessment of five leading city portals. This involved an evaluation of the services hosted on the city portals of Edinburgh, Dublin, Glasgow (Drumchapel), Helsinki (Arabianranta and Munala) and Reykjavic (Garoabaer). The evaluation of the portals included a:

● review of the learning and knowledge services these leading city portals offer stakeholders engaged in digitally inclusive regeneration;
● benchmarking of their existing platforms against the user's knowledge transfer and capacity building requirements;

- selection of the ICTs best able to meet the semantic web requirements of this platform and develop as the natural language of a knowledge-management system supported by a digital library;
- integration of the aforesaid into a platform of e-government services available for members of the communities undergoing such a digitally inclusive regeneration to access as part of their multi-scalar resizing.

This work on digitally inclusive regeneration draws particular attention to the service developments underlying what is referred to as the e-topia demonstrator and citizenship supporting the active participation of communities in this resizing as the recombinant spaces of such a democratic renewal (Deakin, 2009a, 2009b, 2010).

CONCLUSIONS

The aforesaid has carried out an extensive review of Mitchell's thesis on e-topia and found it wanting. The article has pointed out the problems encountered lies with the lack of substantive insight the thesis offers into the embedded intelligence of smart cities.

Although problematic in itself, the article has identified that if the difficulties experienced were only methodological they might perhaps be manageable, but the problem is they run deeper than this and relate to more substantive issues which surround the trajectory of Mitchell's thesis. This is a critical insight of some significance because if the trajectory of the thesis is not in the direction of either the embedded intelligence of smart cities, or the ICTs and digitally inclusive regeneration platforms, then the question arises as to whether the whole notion of e-topia, the cyborg-self and their virtual communities can be a progressive force for change, or merely a way for the embedded intelligence of smart cities to reproduce the status quo. Perhaps more importantly, this in turn begs the question as to whether attempts made to deploy the thesis will prove counter-productive. If in that

sense any attempt to govern the ICTs of digitally inclusive regeneration platforms shall fail because they are unable to be reconciliatory in bridging social divisions and for this very reason do little more than merely add to the inequality of the ecological dis-integration which is already being experienced.

This unfortunate scenario is drawn from what Graham and Marvin have referred to not as e-topia but splintering urbanism, because according to their thesis, the citizenship underlying these communities is no longer able to carry the sheer weight of the material which such a cybernetic-based networking of intelligence is supposed to support. This is important because their scenario has a vision of the future that is the direct opposite of what Mitchell represents and a knowledge base which ends up with cities not so much being smart, as a dumping ground for social inequalities themselves ecologically destructive.

Their representation of splintering urbanism provides what can only be referred to as the antithesis to Mitchell's e-topia. An antithesis that is important because it goes to extreme lengths in searching out, uncovering and exposing the other side of cybernetic-based intelligence which currently lies hidden. It does this by throwing light on the plight of low-income communities living as the urban poor in deprived quarters of the city. From this it is evident that the problems with Mitchell's thesis on e-topia are as much substantive as methodological, the former holding the key to the latter.

In substantive terms this article has gone very much against the grain, arguing that our current understanding of embedded intelligence, smart cities and the ICTs of digitally inclusive regeneration puts us on the verge of a new environmental determinism. An environmental determinism which this time around is cybernetic, based on the embedded intelligence of knowledge-based agents underpinning the networking of smart cities and digitally inclusive regeneration platforms they support. To avoid repeating this mistake (yet) again, attention has been drawn to the work of Graham and Marvin and the spaces which their radical democratic, i.e. egalitarian and ecologically integral, account of the situation opens up for a much more emancipatory view of the intelligence embedded in those knowledge-based agents smart enough to meet these requirements.

Those knowledge-based agents smart enough to meet these requirements and do so by way of and through the social capital underlying and giving rise to the norms, rules and values of such developments. In particular, the social capital that underlies the embedded intelligence of smart cities and which their knowledge-based agents (architects, planners, engineers and surveyors) in turn support by hosting them as services found on digitally inclusive regeneration platforms. Digitally inclusive regeneration platforms whose equity, ecological-integrity and democratic renewal govern over the modernization of villages and neighbourhoods their step-wise logic pave the way for.

In ignoring these warnings and being unable to learn the lessons such a critical reworking of the thesis offers, the strategy Mitchell adopts must be seen as suspect. Not only because the vision and scenarios it advances, also ends up side-stepping such concerns, but for the reason it replaces the agonies of equality and ecological-integrity with the 'gnostics' of 'new age' wordings, centred around storylines about the quality of life. Storylines that spell out, write about and communicate the experiences of those organizations which are wrapped up in such developments.

The strategy advocated for adoption by this article is not grounded in such rhetoric. Its vision of e-topia builds instead on the messages the likes of Graham and Marvin advance by turning the tables and agreeing that: while words offer the possibility of 'bringing what it all means back together', actually turning things around, lies not so much in the words, as it rests with the semantics of the syntax and vocabulary governing the regenerative storylines which emerge from the citizenship (cyborg-civics) of virtual communities and degree to which they

manage to overcome the divided antagonisms of the excluded.

This way it becomes possible for the multiplied memory and infinite mind of the cyborg civic and their tribe-like culture, not to bemoan the nomadicity of wireless bi-peds, but actively celebrate the creativity of the virtual communities emerging from the digital-inclusive nature of such regenerative storylines. In particular celebrate their capacities to be both analytical and synthetic and opportunity this in turn creates for virtual communities to use the collective memory, wikis and blogs of electronically-enhanced services as a means to bridge social divisions.

Bridge them – it is important to note – by drawing upon the political subjectivities of cyborg-civics, their tribe-like culture and nomadicity, as wireless bi-peds with the embedded intelligence smart enough for the citizens of this community to begin spanning such divisions.

Smart enough to begin spanning them and achieve this in a manner which is not merely symbolic, but that is real in the sense which the semantic web of this knowledge-base serves to be the agent of something that is more than a prop. More than a prop and in that sense part of something bigger. Something that is bigger in the sense which any such development allows the wikis and blogs of such web-based services to begin doing the job asked of them. That is the job of building a stage which is large enough for the analytic, synthetic and symbolic to play out the possibilities there are for planning to be both equitable and ecologically integral. Equitable and ecologically integral in the way platforms of this kind allow the cyborg-civics of virtual communities to make all of this real by grasping the potential property development offers them to directly participate in such a digitally inclusive regeneration.

REFERENCES

Brecht, B., 1932, 'The radio as an apparatus of communication', in, J.G. Hanhardt (ed), *Video Culture: A Critical Investigation*, Visual Studies Workshop Press, Rochester, NY.

Calthorpe, P., 1993, *The Next American Metropolis: Ecology, Community, and the American Dream*, Princeton Architectural Press, New York, MIT Press, Cambridge, MA.

Cooper, I., Hamilton, A., Bentivegna, V., 2005, 'Networked communities, virtual organisations and the production of knowledge', in, S. Curwell, M. Deakin, M. Symes (eds), *Sustainable Urban Development Volume 1: The Framework and Protocols for Environmental Assessment*, Routledge, Oxon.

Curwell, S., Deakin, M., Cooper, I., Paskaleva-Shapira, K., Ravetz, J., Babicki, D., 2004, 'Citizens expectations of information cities: implications for urban planning and design', *Building Research and Information* **22**, 1.

Deakin, M., 2009a, 'The IntelCities community of practice: the eGov services model for socially-inclusive and participatory urban regeneration programs', in, C. Reddick (ed), *Handbook of Research on e-Government*, IGI Publishing, Hershey.

Deakin, M., 2009b, 'A community-based approach to sustainable urban regeneration', *Journal of Urban Technology* **16**(1), 191–212.

Deakin, M., 2010, 'Review of city portals: the transformation of service provision under the democratization of the fourth phase', in, C. Reddick (ed), *Politics, Democracy and e-Government: Participation and Service Delivery*, IGI Publishing, Hershey.

Deakin, M., Allwinkle, S., 2006, 'The IntelCities community of practice', *International Journal of Knowledge, Culture and Change Management* **6**(2), 155–162.

Deakin, M., Allwinkle, S., 2007, 'Urban regeneration: the role networks, innovation and creativity play in building successful partnerships', *Journal of Urban Technology* **17**(1), 77–91.

Graham, S., Marvin, S., 1996, *Telecommunications and the City*, Routledge, London.

Graham, S., Marvin, S., 2001, *Splintering Urbanism*, Routledge, London, 2001.

Halpern, D., 2005, *Social Capital*, Policy Press, Bristol.

Horan, T., 2000, *Digital Places: Building Our City of Bits*, Urban Land Institute, Washington, DC.

Katz, P. (ed.), 1993, *New Urbanism: Towards an American Architecture of Community*, McGraw-Hill, New York, NY.

Mitchell, W., 1995, City of Bits: Space, Place, and the Infobahn.

Mitchell, W., 1999, *e-Topia: Urban Life, Jim – But Not as We Know it*, MIT Press, Cambridge, MA.

Mitchell, W., 2001, 'Equitable access to an on-line world', in, D. Schon, B. Sanyal, W.J. Mitchell (eds), *High Technology and Low-Income Communities*, MIT Press, Cambridge, MA.

Mitchell, W., 2004, *Me++: The Cyborg-Self and the Networked City*, MIT Press, Cambridge, MA.

Mitchell, W., 2005, *Placing Words: Symbols, Space, and the City*, MIT Press, Cambridge, MA.

Smart cities, smart places, smart democracy: Form-based codes, electronic governance and the role of place in making smart cities

David Walters

School of Architecture, University of North Carolina at Charlotte, Storrs Hall, 9201 University City Boulevard, Charlotte, NC 28223, USA

Place matters in smart towns and cities. Technology may keep pushing us apart, but we as a culture continue to gather. Opinions differ as to whether the centrifugal forces of 'splintering' urbanism are stronger than the centripetal power of physical places. This article argues that if policies and implementation tools of placed-based urban design are embedded and encoded within the e-governance structure of a community, a balance can be achieved where both physical and virtual realms enhance the unique character of particular locations. The pervasive reach of electronic data and media can help bind the disparate elements of a community together as much as it may seek to disperse them. The process of developing plans, codes and sustainable strategies for a community seeking a truly 'smart' future in a competitive world is illustrated by a case study of Beaufort, a medium-sized town in South Carolina, USA, and these efforts highlight the challenges for English towns and cities in the context of the British Government's shift towards 'localism' in planning.

INTRODUCTION

Place matters in smart towns and cities. 'Smart' in this context can have several interpretations relative to virtual technologies and sustainability, but the simplest and most potent definition of 'place' explains that 'place is space enriched by the assignment of meaning' (Pocock and Hudson, 1978).

While technology keeps pushing us apart, using media to bridge physical distance, we as a culture continue to gather in specific locations that are meaningful to us. The smartest places, therefore, are those that combine the best of both the physical and virtual worlds, where presence and 'tele-presence' are fused together at a location (Mitchell, 1999, p.143). Here, attractive and sustainable physical locations are pervasively penetrated by information and communication technologies (ICTs) to provide a collaborative meshing of physical and virtual environments, with both local and global dimensions. As an antidote to the 'splintering urbanism' suggested by Graham and Marvin (1996,

2001), the centrifugal forces of technology are balanced by centripetal ones of human interaction in physical space.

The techno-topian dimensions of Mitchell's thesis, and the role that fast evolving electronic and computational technologies play in either forming smart cities or destroying urban life is still debatable. This article takes as read that ICTs will continue to evolve in ways that continually challenge our perception and use of space in cities and neighbourhoods and will offer as yet unforeseen new dimensions to patterns of work, living and recreation. There will likely be as many negative as positive outcomes from this technological evolution, and one of the roles of physical, place-based planning and urban design is to capitalize on the positives and offset as many negatives as possible by means of determined, activist and design-based public policies. These major challenges range from counterbalancing the power of global capitalism to create generic 'themed' environments devoid of place-specific design to assisting poor communities in unserviced parts of cities to participate in grassroots regeneration. This theme is examined extensively in the concluding case study of this article.

Whether utopian, dystopian or e-topian, this swirl of techno-futurism will likely leave us even hungrier for some tactile authenticity of place-based experience that only physical locations can supply. In this context, the way cities, towns and neighbourhoods respond to change by managing their physical environments becomes crucial, and it is important to clarify what the adjective 'smart' means in this physical sense so that these attributes can collaborate with their virtual counterparts in creating truly memorable, prosperous and sustainable places.

Walters and Brown (2004, pp.235–236) provide a list of features of smart and sustainable community planning and design, ranging from municipal policies to planning

strategies to detailed urban design concepts. These can be briefly summarized as promoting diverse, compact and mixed-use neighbourhoods that are walkable and transit supportive, with physically defined and accessible public spaces, both urban and natural, and are comprised of energy-efficient buildings that follow the premise of 'long life, loose fit', that is, adaptable to changing patterns of use without major disruption to themselves or their urban surroundings. These principles provide a consistent quality of design and a measure of stability that is the partner in the physical world to the changes and displacements of the virtual world. Increasingly sophisticated information portals and digitally enabled platforms for e-learning, e-governance, community participation and decision making cannot be fully effective in developing truly smart cities and neighbourhoods unless the electronic discourse is underpinned by relevant concepts and tools of physical urban design.

New Urbanism, Smart Growth and sustainable urban design all contain overlapping elements and extensions of this agenda, rooted in the desire to improve the physical design of urban places, enhance social equity and protect the integrity of natural locations. However, one aspect, central to New Urbanism's methodology, is crucial to the process of increasing the 'smartness' of places. Form-based codes (design codes in the UK) are the single most important tool that American planners, urban designers and citizens possess in their efforts to make physical places as smart as possible because they provide the legal armature for the implementation of these physical design principles.

Being smart in this sense does not always come naturally to people or communities; most American planning practices and zoning ordinances of the past 60 years have promoted a much different agenda, one of segregated and dispersed patterns of development that many now brand as physically and socially unsustainable sprawl. But this remains the norm for millions of Americans, and a focused educational and participatory process is afoot within some towns and cities to first raise awareness of the problems with sprawl, secondly to create community plans that capture the vision of a smart(er) future and finally to write the form-based codes, tailored to specific locations, that embed these principles into legal frameworks for implementation. Without smart and sustainable design principles encoded into law, communities wishing to become smart or get smarter (with or without e-learning and digital information platforms) stand little chance of achieving their vision in the chaotic and competitive milieu of social, technical and economic change.

For clarity, the body of the article is divided into four sections as follows:

1 *The role of place in smart communities*: This section examines the continued importance of physical factors in a tele-serviced urbanity, and suggests how particular locations can be enhanced and made unique by a conscious combination of physical and virtual worlds.

2 *Sustainability, 'Smart Growth' and the design of smart places:* Smart places, 'smart growth' and sustainable urbanism are concepts with a great deal of overlap. This section examines the mutual interrelationships between the three approaches and stresses the importance of place-based, participatory design and form-based codes in embedding smart practices within the structure of communities.

3 *Participatory democracy, localism and the role of form-based codes in smart placemaking:* This section considers the implications of the British Coalition Government's determined political shift towards 'localism' in planning and urban development. It examines the role of form-based codes in this new planning regime and compares changes in British practice to equivalent trends in the USA.

4 *Smart and sustainable: a case study of Beaufort, South Carolina, USA:* This case study sets out the democratic process developed by a medium-sized American community to reverse its decline and chart a smart, sustainable future utilizing electronically enhanced 'e-governance'. It explains the role of urban design and form-based codes in bringing about a fusion of the omnipresent and non-place-specific virtual world with the unique character of South Carolina's coastal Low Country.

FIGURE 1 Wireless working in a beautiful place, Dartmouth, Devon, UK. A tourist stepped ashore from his yacht and became a businessman in touch with global networks

THE ROLE OF PLACE IN SMART COMMUNITIES

There is a consistent and basic human need to belong somewhere, and 'there is no reason to believe that this need will disappear as a result of increased electronic connectivity' (Mitchell,

1999, p.73). On the contrary, when we can live and work anywhere we choose, we select places that please, support and nurture us on several levels. Pocock and Hudson's definition of place enlarges the concept from simply a physical location to a more complex socio-spatial construct that can embody different meanings for different people. As such, placemaking factors are crucial elements of a space's identity and unique character that defines it from other locations that might compete for our attention, activity and business (Figures 1 and 2).

While virtual media are vital elements for places to be successful, they themselves are not respecters of location. Left to their own devices, one tele-serviced spot is as good as another, with convenience perhaps the only moderator. For locations to become places in the more meaningful sense, to hold some special status in our cultural hierarchy, they have to combine the convenience of global linkage in the virtual realm with characterful physical presence, and that comes chiefly through the quality of urban design.

The technological challenge currently posed to traditional urban space by virtual media is not the first one in the history of the modern city. One needs to look back only to 1964, when Melvin Webber (1963, 1964) published two

FIGURE 2 The Dartmouth Estuary. Devon, UK. The beautiful physical setting of Dartmouth is increasingly a place of global connectivity

influential articles entitled *The Urban Place and the Nonplace Urban Realm* and *Order in Diversity: Community without Propinquity*. Webber rejected models of the city based on traditional spatial patterns and argued that it was a mistake to critique the expanding city as shapeless sprawl, or to long instead for traditional streets and squares, because the car had changed the relationship between space and time in cities. Propinquity, being near everything one needed, was no longer a necessity for mobile families; instead of defined physical places in the traditional townscape of spatial enclosure and walking distances, the new city was based on a pattern of dispersal, where individuals and families constructed their sense of the city from a series of physically discontinuous locations, connected only by driving.

The real point of Webber's thesis, however, was not simply that it was possible to move around easily to lots of different places, but that at a deep, fundamental level *place did not matter anymore* (Walters and Brown, 2004, p.23). Instead of community being grounded in a particular location, and experienced within an integrated hierarchy of meaningful places and neighbourhoods, a new pattern of social relationships could be created from weaving together the disparate strands of daily life from a variety of generic locations. The city became a non-hierarchical network where locations were equalized by their accessibility by car. In this context, argued Webber, traditional urban forms were simply irrelevant.

This shifting equation between propinquity and accessibility has remained a central issue for architects, planners, geographers and cultural critics (Sennett, 1971, 1974; Castells, 1989, 1997; Harvey, 1989; Soja, 1989; Jameson, 1991; Sassen, 1991; Howell, 1993; Mitchell, 1995, 1999, 2001; Watson and Gibson, 1995; Graham and Marvin, 1996, 2001; Kelly, 1998; Gilder, 2000). Some suggested that traditional community life was obsolete, and that the virtual space of ever expanding social media had forever replaced physical space as the primary medium of personal, commercial and cultural dialogue, rendering traditional urban places outdated at an even more fundamental level than Webber predicted. In a time when Facebook and Twitter were unknown, Michael Dear went so far as to say that 'the phone and the modem have rendered the street irrelevant' (Dear, 1995, p.31).

However, other critics were quick to make the counter-argument: in a society that enables us to live and work anywhere we like, the places we choose to inhabit become all the more precious and important. Sassen argued persuasively in *The Global City* (1991; 2nd ed 2002) that the global economy, far from being placeless, needed very specific 'territorial insertions', and that this need was sharpest within highly globalized and electronic sectors such as finance. Cultural critics who subscribed to 'human capital theory', such as Lucas (1988), Kotkin (2001) and Florida (2002) noted that wealth accumulated wherever 'intelligence clusters' evolved, and that groupings of creative and productive innovators were the main impetus of place-specific urban development and wealth creation. Mitchell (1999, p.155) asserts that as 'traditional locational imperatives weaken, we will gravitate to settings that offer particular

FIGURE 3 Totnes, Devon, UK. The medieval town of Totnes has become a leader in the 'Transition Town' movement towards self-reliant localism in culture, energy and food

cultural, scenic and climatic attractions – those unique qualities that cannot be pumped through a wire – together with those face-to-face interactions we care most about.'

We are all familiar with generic locations for meetings, accommodations and entertainment where the locale is disappointingly forgettable. But in more satisfying scenarios, this globally driven, ICT-infused urbanity can interact with local history, geography, culture, politics and economics to produce diversified places where localism is a valued partner and counterpoint to globalism. Beyond superficial symbolism and touristic hype, the most profound localisms are likely to be based around local production of culture, energy and food, giving a sustainable edge to the local character of each successful place. The Transition Town Movement, for example, begun in Kinsale, Ireland and in Totnes, England in 2005–06, embodies the emerging principles and practices of transitioning from a globalized, high-carbon environment to a more localized, self-sufficient and low-carbon alternative (Hopkins, 2008). This local presence combines with tele-presence, where physical space is penetrated by the virtual spaces of community e-learning portals and digital platforms, to considerable mutual benefit.

One can quite easily imagine a 'Transition Town', successfully rooted in its physical location and adapting to a low-carbon future while seamlessly tele-serviced with global connectivity. Totnes, for example, is a beautiful and historic market town surrounded by lush and productive countryside, a privileged setting for its 'Energy Descent Action Plan' (http://totnesedap.org.uk/) (Figure 3). However, there will be many other locations unable to adapt easily to future paradigms bred from changes in technology, energy production and climate. These less fortunate communities, large and small, will likely decline unless sterling public policy initiatives and determined grassroots regeneration efforts combine in both the physical and virtual worlds.

There are thus huge and problematic issues of social equity and economic sustainability inherent in these potential future patterns. At worst, such forces could combine to reinforce the incipient and troubling caste system already evident within some American locations, where upper echelon workers and residents are supported by lower-level service populations who cannot afford to live where they work and who are forced instead to subsist in distant, second-rate bedroom communities.

It is clear, then, that far from ameliorating divisions within our culture, developments in ICT have the propensity to reinforce existing fissure lines within society, and deliberate public policy initiatives are required to counteract these 'splintering' effects, not least in terms of housing affordability, employment opportunities and balanced, diverse communities, all key elements of sustainable places.

SUSTAINABILITY AND THE DESIGN OF SMART PLACES

Public policies to promote these smart, sustainable outcomes in the longer term often run counter to local prejudice based on short-term and status quo thinking. While community-based digital platforms can be useful tools in promoting education and debate, the anonymity provided by electronic discourse also allows for a viral coarsening of debate and a polarization of opinion. (This is clear by a quick review of online commentary in any American regional newspaper, e.g. where community debate is usually reduced to a series of unpleasant posts insulting all who think differently from the anonymous correspondent.)

It is thus very helpful for the main forums of public debate about smart planning and design to retain a major face-to-face component, using such vehicles as design charrettes in America, and Enquiry by Design forums in the UK (Walters, 2007). The aim here is to increase civility and transparency while partnering with blogs and wiki sites set up for each project; the goal is *not* to produce consensus (nice in theory but often impossible in practice), but to ensure that all points of view are openly expressed and noted, so that when decisions are taken by elected representatives, no citizen can say that they were denied an opportunity to state their opinion.

The goal in these public forums is to move beyond the discussion of generic planning principles, however well intentioned they may be, and illustrate issues by place-specific design proposals using both traditional and digital media. Smart towns and cities achieve their status primarily through good, place-specific and participatory urban design that mediates both local and global forces, and this complexity can best be handled by detailed design examples directly relevant to the community. Urban design representations in two and three dimensions can defuse NIMBY-style opposition to sustainable policies far more effectively than abstract diagrams of those same planning concepts (Figure 4).

Even when good urban design for smart communities has the public's blessing at its inception, it is not realized by simply hoping that architects and developers will implement it. Appropriate standards of sustainable urbanism need to be required and incentivized. One of the most effective means of achieving these desired outcomes is the use of 'form-based codes' in the USA, or 'design codes' in England.[1] Instead of the conventional development approach based on separated single uses – housing here, offices over there and no mixing of functions, for example – form-based codes (a key product of New Urbanism in the USA[2]) use time-tested urban morphologies and typologies to legislate for an integrated, sustainable and holistic future environment.

A tele-serviced and place-specific future demands more of cities, towns and neighbourhoods than generic use-based codes can supply. Such codes have been instrumental in turning American suburbia into

FIGURE 4 Town Centre redevelopment proposal, Huntersville, North Carolina. (by The Lawrence Group). Representations in two and especially three dimensions can defuse NIMBY-style opposition to proposals for sustainable development far more effectively than abstract diagrams of those same planning concepts. Here, a new town center complex sits adjacent to a planned commuter rail station

a placeless, monotonous landscape for the past 60 years, and have created disconnected, auto-dominated environments that appear increasingly unsustainable in the face of looming global challenges. In a globalized world, uses overlap and change quickly, and adaptability becomes a highly prized urban virtue. In this context, single use zoning is beyond obsolete; it can be actively harmful to the economic future of towns and cities.

How we make gathering spaces – focal places in our communities – is thus very important. Ancient Romans believed that each particular place had a characteristic spirit – its *genius loci* – and in the context of today's continuingly evolving digital environment, part of this genius is now manifested by the pervasive infiltration of software computer code, augmenting the local place with global connectivity. Mitchell suggests this code can give 'character' to a place by encoding rules and protocols that facilitate some activities and discourage others (Mitchell, 1999, p.50). By

direct analogy, form-based or design codes, created within a participatory democratic process, 'encode' the physical environment. They can encourage or mandate key aspects of sustainable, smart community design while disallowing other patterns that erode community character and would otherwise perpetuate practices that waste energy and resources. A combination of the two types of codes, with form-based codes embedded within the e-governance structure of a community, can thus create 'interlinked, interacting ... smart, attentive and responsive places' (Mitchell, 1999, p.68).

While it is necessary for globalized connectivity to complement local character in creating sustainable, smart places, other aspects of global culture, allied with corporate capital, can also produce their antithesis – a deadening sameness of formulaic or faux 'themed' environments everywhere. In this context of resistance to generic forces and the highlighting of place-specific counterpoints, form-based codes have become the tool of choice for the creation of smart places. In almost all cases, these codes have been products of New Urbanist theory and practice, and have sought from the outset to respect and enhance the characteristics of the particular places where they are used. Most form-based codes are much more respectful of the natural environment than conventional, use-based ordinances, and this environmental impetus has increased over the years of their use. As issues of sustainability in smart communities become more widely recognized, the emphasis placed on the longevity and adaptability of building forms and urban spaces in design codes becomes a positive factor in sustainable design: when buildings are more durable, they are adaptable to change and there is a longer period of time over which the environmental impact of the buildings and the energy used in their construction can be spread (Symes and Pauwells, 1999, p.104).

The history, development and operation of form-based codes in Britain and America have been documented by Walters and Brown (2004), Walters (2007) and in the purely American context by Parolek et al. (2008). Several key points were learned from the process of creating early codes in the 1980s and 1990s, especially the relationship between urban morphology (the sense of overall grain and character of an urban area) and building typology (a lexicon of different types of buildings based on their formal characteristics). This renewed interest in traditional urban forms of public space (street, square, alley, park, etc.) and neighbourhood layout, (connected streets, grids, mixed uses, etc.) suggested a way of coding based on hierarchical spatial zones of urban or rural character rather than specified uses, and these 'character zones' dictated the overall scale and arrangement of building types within their areas (Keane and Walters, 1995, Town of Davidson). Within this morphological urban categorization, form-based codes regulated new development by building types (with flexible patterns of use), design standards for streets, parking areas and public open spaces and by provisions covering landscape and signage.

This same logic forms the basis of the subsequent 'Transect' methodology developed by Duany and Plater-Zyberk in the late 1990s, and now widely used in urban design and progressive planning practice across the USA. This Transect is an environmental ordering system conceptualized as a long section through an idealized landscape from rural edge to city centre (Duany Plater-Zyberk (DPZ), 2002), and owes a debt to the classic valley section of Scottish geographer Patrick Geddes (1915), which set the various sectors of urbanization in their regional geographic context.

Geddes and other users of similar concepts utilized the technique to describe existing situations (Conzen, 1968; Coleman, 1978). In contrast, New Urbanists use the Transect to describe the way things *ought to be* (Brower, 2002, p.314). This use of urban design concepts and categories of urban or rural character to define and manage the future is characteristic of most form-based zoning codes; however, the key to the current Transect, as with the earlier Town of Davidson example lies in giving legal weight to concepts of morphological urban analysis.

The Transect (such as the methodology used in the Case Study section of this article) draws a cross section through an imaginary landscape, identifying six types of environmental zones, each defined by its morphological character, and moving from T1 (rural preserve) through ascending scales of suburban and urban areas leading to the densest area T6 (urban core) (Figure 5). A seventh classification, an 'assigned' or 'specialized district', exists for non-urban uses such as airports, landfills and the like that do not fit easily into urban or suburban zones.

This hierarchical scale enables urban designers, planners and the public to see the

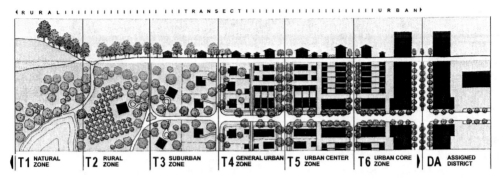

FIGURE 5 Transect diagram. This version of the transect, developed by the architecture and planning firm Duany Plater-Zyberk, Inc., has become a model for progressive town planning and urban design methods in the USA

various kinds of rural and urban landscape as a continuum that relates different types of urbanity to the ecological factors of particular zones. This morphological thinking is then transferred from the hypothetical landscape to the exact particulars of the specific location under consideration, setting out an overall planning strategy for the community.

In an attempt to standardize principles of good urban design and sustainable development, Duany and Plater-Zyberk initiated the Smart Code in the USA in the late 1990s as an evolving experiment to formalize the planning and design principles of the Transect methodology into a comprehensive zoning ordinance that could be customized, or 'calibrated' for any municipality. Now in Version 9.2 (2010), the Smart Code aims to integrate urban design principles, basic architectural controls, public works standards, zoning and subdivision regulations into a single unified ordinance spanning scales from the region, the community, the urban block and the building, in keeping with the principles of the Charter of the New Urbanism. According to the Smart Code Complete website, as of August 2010, there were 332 codes in the USA that meet form-based criteria, plus an additional 11 form-based guidelines. In all, 101 of these were adopted, with the others in progress. While this represents a substantial achievement in improved zoning practice in

the USA, it constitutes only a very small proportion of American municipalities, indicating just how few towns and cities have regulations in place that will assist in future transitions to truly smart communities (www.smartcodecomplete.com/learn/links.html).

In England, the introduction of design codes as part of national policy is relatively new (Carmona and Dann, 2007a; Walters, 2007). The Labour Government's Planning Guidance Note 3 (DETR, 2000) provided endorsement of design codes, related to that Government's long-term ambition to create sustainable communities and meet the increasing demand for new homes in England. The policy was further developed through Labour's Sustainable Communities Plans (ODPM, 2005a, b), which contained the implicit assumption that new delivery mechanisms, including some form of design coding, were required to achieve the challenging targets for housing. Following the launch of the Sustainable Communities Plan, the Government, working in partnership with CABE (the Commission for Architecture and the Built Environment, a national body charged with upholding design standards for new development) and English Partnerships (the national development and urban regeneration agency since absorbed within the Government's Homes and Communities Agency), instituted a research programme to allow design codes to be tested in practice (Carmona and Dann, 2007b, www. rudi.net/books/15899).

In the light of the new Coalition Government's radical budget cuts and planning proposals that have defunded CABE, scrapped national housing targets and ridiculed the Labour Government's planning policies and detailed guidance notes that focused heavily on design codes as 'Soviet tractor-style top-down planning' (Sayer, 2010, p.14), there is uncertainty regarding the future of design coding in England. This is examined further in 'Participatory Democracy, Localism, and the Role of Form-Based Codes in Smart Placemaking' section below, which compares possible outcomes to current American practice. A more detailed examination of progressive American practice is then described in the concluding Case Study section.

PARTICIPATORY DEMOCRACY, LOCALISM AND THE ROLE OF FORM-BASED CODES IN SMART PLACEMAKING

The principle that people who use public spaces and buildings should have a say in designing them is central to the notion of an enhanced, smart community. In America this belief represents a fundamental tenet of New Urbanism as the Preamble to *The Charter of the New Urbanism* clearly states: 'We are committed to reestablishing the relationship between the art of building and the making of community, through citizen-based participatory planning and design' (CNU, 2000, p.iv). Contemporaneous British government documents such as *By design: urban design in the planning system: towards better practice* make this point equally forcefully: 'It is not enough to consult people about decisions that will impact on their lives: they must be fully engaged from the start' (DETR and CABE, 2000, p.32).

This same conviction is expressed (in what promises to be a radically different form) in new policy guidelines set out by the Conservative and Liberal Democrat Coalition Government's planning proposals highlighted in the consultative Green Paper, *Open Source Planning* (Conservative Party (UK), 2010). Here the emphasis shifts from regional and central government to local community controls of planning and development, and new development can be fast-tracked for approval if an effective public design charrette such as the British 'Enquiry By Design' process has been used.

The main difference between planning for sustainable communities in Britain and America had been that American initiatives tend to be very localized, the result of individual towns and cities trying to establish a sophisticated framework for growth management with little coordinated help from federal or state government. In Britain, in contrast, three design disciplines – urban design, transportation design and environmental design – had for more than a decade been specifically incorporated into the Labour government's national policies.

At first glance, the new Coalition Government's proposals for 'open source, localized planning' seem to move English planning practice sharply towards the largely ineffective American model where little regional organization exists, and local governments are left to fend for themselves in a competitive quest for resources.

Concerns about the loss of integrated regional planning were expressed directly by Ann Skipton, the President of the Royal Town Planning Institute, who suggested that the move towards localism put Britain's economic recovery at risk. Skipton added that strategic regional planning was 'vital' as the coordinating level between national and local governments to ensure proper coordination across municipal boundaries (Sayer, 2010, p.16). Despite this passionate argument, the Coalition government's Minister for Local Government, Eric Pickles, moved quickly to dismantle the regional planning structure across England. In its place the Government's Green Paper outlines the vague objective of 'bringing communities together, as they formulate a shared vision of sustainable development' (p.1) and proposes a 'Duty to Co-operate' (p.3) on all local planning authorities and other public bodies to avoid uncoordinated development.

The future and role of design codes within a less coordinated planning system in England remains an unresolved question. Currently, the use of design codes in the UK is not mandatory; rather they are used at the discretion of local planning authorities and/or developers. Successful codes, such as the well-known example at Upton, in Northampton, function largely as mechanisms that can raise the standards of urban design and development by specifying clear urban design principles and detailing requirements for the built environment.

Code preparation is a skilled and time-intensive task, and it is not clear who will fund this process, what the scope of such codes might be and what geographic area they might cover. Nor is it clear if local governments will have either the professional staff to develop and administer sophisticated, design-based development control measures or if they will have sufficient resources to hire private consultants for these tasks in a time of stringent budget cuts. However, if resources are available, this move towards localism does represents an opportunity for urban designers to play a role within their communities in terms of creating and monitoring development proposals, and promoting the agendas of smart and sustainable communities.

In the context of British right-wing Conservative policies focused on reducing the size and scope of government and promoting business-led economic development, it is ironic to note that much of the content of the Green Paper places it well to the left-of-centre in the current American political spectrum. Sustainable development is a mantra that permeates the Conservatives' document, with acknowledgement of standards for environmental, social and economic sustainability, the need for renewable energy generation requirements, along with Green Belt protection, and the need for planning controls to 'stop unsustainable suburban sprawl'. The document also notes the requirement for developers to pay 'a tariff that compensates the community for loss of amenity and costs of additional infrastructure' (Conservative Party (UK), 2010, p.3).

Such a tariff equates to American 'impact fees', one of the few 'smart growth' mechanisms American municipalities have to offset the costs to towns and cities of new development. These fees link urban growth to the provision of adequate public facilities, such as larger schools, more parks and libraries, demanded by the new residents. Without impact fees, these costs have to be borne (some say unfairly) by existing residents in the form of higher property taxes. Such fees are trenchantly opposed by right-wing American think-tanks on ideological grounds, along with most builders and developers who seek to divest themselves of the responsibility of any costs for new facilities. While grudgingly ruled legal in some states, courts in other states, such as North Carolina, have barred their use, thus depriving local authorities of a useful tool in the fight for sustainable development. In most American states today, the British Conservatives' policies would be looked on as a dangerous form of socialism, to be defeated at all costs.

Regardless of how the new Coalition Government politics play out at home, both English and American practice to date has shown that there is still a major role for design codes within both planning systems. In a hopeful sign that this might continue, the Green Paper specifically states (p.10) that:

The quality of the built environment is crucial in creating liveable communities. We want to encourage the creation of buildings which are practical, sustainable, affordable and attractive, and also deliver social goals, for instance by 'designing out' crime. We must promote the highest standards of architecture and design. ... We will therefore expect local authorities to set out architectural and design standards in their local plans.

It is therefore possible that design codes will continue to play an important role in English planning practice and the quest for smart, sustainable communities. Further clarity is needed to determine how design codes can be used effectively to promote innovation and creativity, and their relationship with sustainability measures. Codes should be based on sound sustainability principles, resourced appropriately by skilled, multi-disciplinary professionals and given appropriate time for formulation, adoption and implementation. These latter tasks can be greatly facilitated by using smart ICT platforms and portals.

In the context of this new 'localism' emphasis in English community planning and design, and the apparent move towards a more American condition of local initiatives without the benefit of clear regional structure and priorities, it is instructive to review an American example of a once declining town now taking charge of its smarter and more

FIGURE 6 Beaufort, South Carolina. Old homes, wide porches and Spanish Moss dripping from live oak trees provide the romantic character of Beaufort's town center

sustainable future. Against an American backdrop of budget cuts, a growing resistance towards funding for infrastructure, a profound distaste for regional planning and collaborative government, and great suspicion about global warming (it is a socialist plot against American prosperity! [www.examiner.com/liberal-issues-in-national/sarah-palin-sees-global-warming-as-socialist-plot-commentary]), the narrative of Beaufort, South Carolina, provides an optimistic and emerging smart alternative to current 'head in the sand' attitudes of many Americans.[3]

Without being aware of the fact, many readers of this article likely know Beaufort, SC (pronounced B-YEW-fort). It was the setting for the famous 1983 movie, *The Big Chill* – depicted as a sleepy Southern, riverfront city with live oak-lined streets and 19th century mansions (Figure 6). Early Spanish and French explorers contested the region, with its fine natural harbour, from the 16th century onwards, until British colonists settled the land early in the 18th century, despite resistance by the native Yemassee Indians.

Its compact network of streets was laid out from 1711 onwards, and named after a British aristocrat, Henry Somerset, Duke of Beaufort, one of the eight Lords Proprietors of Carolina who administered the colony for the British Crown. The first town plan comprised 397 lots and a public square, sited on the higher ground between the confluence of two rivers – the Broad River to south and the Beaufort River to the north. Located equidistant between the larger and now more globally prominent Charleston, SC, and Savannah, GA, Beaufort has preserved elements of its history, sometimes intentionally, sometimes by neglect, and is now aggressively preparing for its next stage of evolution into a smart and sustainable community.

The economy of Beaufort, largely founded on the plantation labour of African slaves until the American Civil War (1861–65), is now predominately based on tourism and government. The largest employers are the military (Marine Corps Recruit Station-Parris Island and Marine Corps Air Station-Beaufort), the Beaufort County school district, the University of South Carolina-Beaufort and ... Wal-Mart. Parris Island attracts more than 17,000 recruits annually for the 13-week Marine Corps basic training and fills short-term housing and hotel rooms for visiting family and friends, while the Air Station is a much more stable element in the local economy. This branch of the military comes with longer-term base assignments, higher-paying officer jobs and a large number of civilian support positions.

But as this small city enters its 4th century (a long time for American towns), the challenges before it have rarely been greater. The county school system remains under a federal order to ensure racial balance and the city's infrastructure has long been feeling its age with inconsistent maintenance through a lack of leadership and resources. Combined with disinvestment in the historic city core, the policies of past decades promoted generic suburban development in the environmentally fragile greenfields and marsh areas around the town, resulting in a sense of mediocre placelessness, in keeping with much of contemporary America.

In contrast, all the discussions in this article have been predicated upon the opposite point of view: place matters, especially in an e-connected world. Beaufort's leaders now recognize that to renew itself and to recreate prosperity, the town has to capitalize on its unique qualities of place and its ability to provide the kind of highly serviced, active urban lifestyle in a beautiful setting sought after by a wide range of demographic groups.

Compact, walkable districts with a mix of uses and a range of live-work and housing options create environments more conducive to, and supportive of tele-connected working and living than does low-density suburbia, and Beaufort's historic core acts handily as the model for future development. Its physical, place-centred attributes now drive new development standards, embedded into a developing ICT environment supported by the city through its Digital City Hall and the newly created Office of Civic Investment, charged with planning Beaufort's future.

These portals provide electronically enhanced representations of Beaufort's public services such as police and public works, economic and workforce development, planning, urban design and housing, transportation, tourism and recreation – that is, all those elements within the city's purview needed to sustain a good quality of life in the community. (Other community services such as education and libraries are handled by Beaufort County.) In particular, the portals set up a framework for electronically enhanced 'e-governance' and community participation in planning that integrates the virtual realm and the physical world of master plans and form-based codes.

The electronic planning portal offers a vision of the future able to sustain the city: a progressive comprehensive plan is underpinned by the Transect and an ongoing series of neighbourhood sector plans and form-based codes are developed through democratic, public and electronically enhanced design charrettes for maximum citizen participation. These improvements to local planning content and practice are framed within a revised Unified Development Ordinance (UDO) that provides quick electronic access to local data, global links and application information.

The process of transforming Beaufort into a physically smart and sustainable place began in earnest in 2005–6 with the Boundary Street Master Plan for one of the main highway corridors into the historic core. In a straightforward application of New Urbanist principles, the plan's goal was to replace an unsightly mish-mash of strip development with a memorable entrance to the town that did justice to its historic physical setting. One key element was a new form-based code derived directly from the master plan as the mechanism to orchestrate implementation, and phases 1 and 2 are expected to be complete in 2012 and 2013.

Worthy as this plan was, it dealt piecemeal with one particular set of problems, and the following year, Beaufort participated in the much larger Northern Beaufort County Regional Plan (2007), involving also Beaufort County, the neighbouring Town of Port Royal, and the Marine Corps Air Station-Beaufort. This plan set forth a new, coordinated framework of development by establishing clear growth boundaries, a coherent regional structure, a coordinated conservation and transportation vision, and a fiscal strategy that assessed the cost of unchecked suburban sprawl. This process began a much-needed regional conversation between the four participating organizations about leadership, governance and development than has begun (finally) to foster collaborative planning for the greater common good.

Maintaining momentum, the City of Beaufort commissioned a community-wide Smart Growth Audit in 2008 to assess Beaufort's then-current growth policies and implementation measures against the accepted principles of Smart Growth and sustainable development. This highlighted several opportunities for improvements in policies and design standards, and set the scene for *Vision Beaufort*, a Comprehensive Plan from the Lawrence Group that established new sustainable development priorities and metrics for the whole city. At the heart of the Comprehensive Plan lies the Framework Plan based on the Transect methodology and related form-based code classifications. The Framework Plan focuses on environmental protection and clustering development into walkable, mixed-use nodes, which are explored and illustrated in 2- and 3-D design detail prior to coding. These design exercises for specific sites, tied to code provisions, promote placemaking by ensuring that future development respects the character and qualities of each locality while incorporating progressive agendas for social inclusiveness,

diversity and housing affordability. By doing so, they create the potential environments that can reverse previous negative trends and attract new residents and workers (Figure 7).

The Comprehensive and Framework Plans set the context for more detailed plans and place-specific form-based codes. One such plan and code has been developed for a major street through the historic core (the Bladen Street Plan and form-based code, 2010), and at the time of writing in early 2011 a draft county-wide form-based code has been produced which will be locally calibrated in each jurisdiction by public design charrettes for neighbourhoods and districts beginning in Beaufort with the Sector 1 Plan described below.

These efforts in local, place-based urban regeneration were made possible by determined political leadership, a very competent municipal planning staff, sufficient resources to hire high-caliber consultants, and a commitment to developing an ICT infrastructure for enhanced civic discourse. Above all, however, was a belief that this combination of electronic media and place-based urban design could be the agents of community bonding, bringing the community together around their unique location, its history and a compelling vision for its future through an extensive Civic Master Planning process. .

For a small city such as Beaufort (population 12,235 in 2010), which missed out on many growth opportunities during the last decade due to uninspired public policies and poor-quality infrastructure, this planning process represents a major economic development tool, used to reposition the city as a progressive community and to package development opportunities that are market ready yet sensitive to place, history and context. Place-based components are heavily emphasized as an antidote to the generic quality of contemporary development and this place-based focus is embedded into the process of crafting the form-based code, its

FIGURE 7 Beaufort Framework Plan detail. Design exercises for specific sites explain proposals clearly and become the basis for much electronic discourse and the development of form-based codes tailored to particular places

content and its digital presence in the virtual world.

The case study indicates the complexity of the tasks facing communities in America, and the level of professional resources needed to create sustainable, smart futures in the face of technological, economic and political forces that can easily lead to the 'splintering' or fragmentation of places and their communities. These challenges are considerable, as the progressive agenda of Transect-based master plans and form-based codes described here is not the norm in the USA, either politically or professionally. It is not enough just to care about places; hard work must ensue to embed their unique characteristics in plans and place-specific codes. Then further effort is required to implant this methodology firmly within the electronic discourse of the community. At that point, towns and cities become smart.

As part of Beaufort's multi-year Civic Master Planning process, and following on from the 2009 Comprehensive Plan, the town has been divided into five separate planning sectors for detailed study over two to three years. As noted by Beaufort's Office of Civic Investment, each Sector Plan will comprise the following elements:

- Physical development and redevelopment plans to the parcel level illustrating the preferred lot arrangements, building typologies and frontages.
- Physical infrastructure plans illustrating preferred street sections for all streets and required improvements.
- Natural systems plans illustrating preferred stormwater management techniques, open-space protection/preservation, water access, watercourse buffers and other natural areas.
- Civic infrastructure plans that identify opportunities to improve, expand and/or inject new community facilities and

amenities into each sector in a manner that creates a coherent and distinctive armature for the entire community.

- Designation of specific sending and receiving areas to implement a regional Transfer of Development Rights (TDR) programme (using work created by others and locally calibrated).
- Civic investment strategies that identify capital and operating needs for each sector and prioritize improvements and investments.
- Calibration of the county-wide form-based code to the block-level in Beaufort.
- Extensive illustrations providing a visual palette from which to market various development and redevelopment opportunities at a parcel level to a variety of developers and development agencies.

The Civic Master Plan aims to establish principles and standards that all public and private development will follow; effectively it will encode the community's physical and cultural DNA for all future development. The city's Office of Civic Investment will identify and promote investment and reinvestment opportunities, block by block, in each neighbourhood throughout the entire city. Each neighbourhood has its history, unique character and physical attributes that the plans will respect, build upon, enhance and encode. The Civic Master Plan will be very visual with extensive 2- and 3-D graphic representations, and will give residents and businesses a clear picture of what is intended. As such, it will serve as a physical and digital tool to use to stimulate various development and/or redevelopment opportunities throughout Beaufort.

The specificity of the whole study area for Sector 1, the first in the planning series and covering an area of a little more than one square mile (approx. 2.7 km^2), was recorded in comprehensive detail in a data bank of all properties within the study area. This data bank, available online through the charrette's website, comprised information on every building's location, use, condition, style and ownership or rental status, all available digitally for professionals, the public and elected officials. This enabled the designs, and the codes developed from them, to be crafted in very fine grain and with great specificity for the particulars of place. The comprehensiveness and accessibility of the virtual database extends the on-site reality of each planning area for smooth operational transitions between physical and digital realms and for easy sharing of information among team members and the public. In this way, the worlds of physical and digital reality become complementary and interpenetrating.

At the time of writing the first detailed calibration of the county-wide form-based code was partly complete with a week-long and highly public charrette involving a team of 25 urban designers, planners and transportation experts. This intensive design process followed months of face-to-face public meetings, plus blogs and an extensive digital discourse through the community and beyond via the city's Office of Civic Investment website:beaufortcivicinvestment.org/.

The local calibration was structured from a set of design and development proposals crafted on a block-by-block (sometimes a lot-by-lot) basis throughout the historic downtown and early-20th-century town extensions all located on the town's geographic peninsula (see Figure 8). Once these proposals were honed through the public debate process of the charrette with detailed local input from citizens, the county-wide code's transect categories were recalibrated into sub-sections for precise tailoring to the desired urban conditions for that charrette area, and a new, Transect-based regulating plan produced with T-zone categories ranging from varieties of T3 small-scale neighbourhood to denser T5 urban and historic cores (see Figure 9). The full form-based code for this historic area of Beaufort is currently under production for further public debate and council approval.

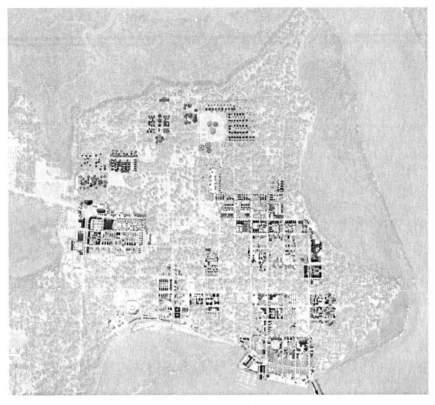

FIGURE 8 Beaufort Sector 1 Urban Design Plan. This illustrates the complete range of potential development proposals as the basis of form based code calibration

The lessons from this case study point one clear way forward in the ongoing discussions regarding the relationships between real places and virtual worlds in the arena of community design. It is advantageous to take the time required to record and analyse the detailed specifics of the planning project's location so as to create a virtual lexicon of built and natural components the physical place. This is time intensive during the analysis and preparation stages of the work but very valuable during the fast-paced and complex design charrette process. The immediate electronic presence of draft designs from the charrette on local websites can thus be referenced back to details of the physical location with relative ease and the proposed changes, together with an existing information base can be widely distributed for commentary and advice.

This gives rise to a productive conjunction of media, place and distance. Much of the work in the charrette studio is very traditional – hand drawing and colouring on trace paper over large aerial photographs in front of the public, who comment extensively over the designers' shoulders. This traditional format provides a valuable immediacy between designers and the public that is essential to any successful charrette. It truly roots the process in place.

These hand drawings are then combined with normative computer graphic media to produce a series of hybrid presentations, both time and place specific to the charrette and digitally available in the virtual realm, thus blurring time and space to invite wider

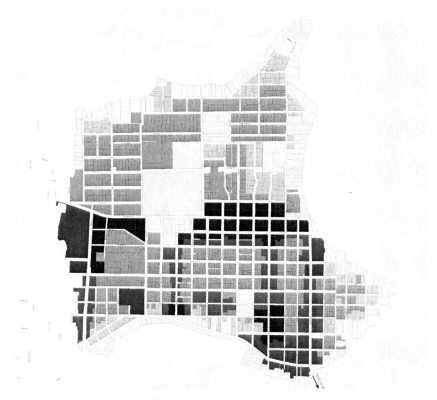

FIGURE 9 This Transect-based Regulating Plan replaces a patchwork of conventional use-based zoning categories with a hierarchical series of low- to high-density mixed-use urban neighbourhoods

commentary and input. But the charrette itself is only part of the process: it sets the project specific plans in place as the illustrative basis for detailed form-based code elaborations that can be properly detailed relative to physical and historical circumstances. The digital encoding of these form-based specifics thus fixes the physicality of Beaufort in the virtual realm. What exists digitally is predicated on the specifics of the place – existing and proposed. And what exists physically on the ground together with the specific outlines of future development projects is translated seamlessly and embedded into the digital world. There is no tension or mismatch between the two realms: no fragmentation or splintering. The same place-based DNA is encoded in both realms by the digital

manifestation of the place-specific form-based code.

CONCLUSION

Debate continues to swirl around the relevance of traditionally construed physical places as settings for human activity and discourse in a world both expanded and collapsed by digital media. Mitchell's view of a potentially fruitful and mutually beneficial collaboration between the physical and virtual worlds sits in contrast to Graham and Marvin's more dystopian vision of a world splintered and fragmented by technological mobilities and networked infrastructures. This latter view suggests that fast-developing 'electronic consumption and surveillance systems … threaten to provide silent, invisible and pervasive networks …

with unprecedented potential for exclusion' (Graham and Marvin, 2001, p.383). The implication is clear: if 'place' matters at all, such well-designed locations will likely be the realm of the more privileged classes. Those that do not fit some approved demographic profile can be denied admittance.

In the face of this critique, this article has argued that Mitchell's position has continued relevance, particularly if the process of place-based urban design is rooted in participatory democracy, utilizes electronic media to structure and extend democratic debate and, most importantly, creates clear implementation strategies and regulations through the use of form-based or design coding. Designing neighbourhood and community plans in detail and in open democratic forums, encoding these design principles into easily understood form-based regulations, and making these easily accessible via electronic portals facilitates both the process of community building and the broad dissemination of important, locally focused information.

There is no denying the power of Graham and Marvin's alternative view that the increasing 'privatization and liberalization of infrastructure systems' is unravelling the city as a place where people come together for common purposes, and implanting instead conditions of spatial segregation, social polarization and exclusion (Graham and Marvin, 2001, p.383). Against this proposition, the City of Beaufort, SC, stands as a place of resistance to these trends, using electronic media and its content as agents of social and physical cohesion.

Graham and Marvin suggest, quite rightly, that traditional urban master plans should be treated with skepticism because they can fix exclusionary policies in time and place to the detriment of certain societal groups. The inclusionary, democratic process used by Beaufort in its planning activities seeks to mitigate this concern, going out of its way to enhance public input through charrette-based blogs and online community discussions. By a clearly stated commitment in the 2007 Comprehensive Plan to the 'triple bottom line' of economic prosperity, environmental stewardship and social justice, derived from the preceding Smart Growth and sustainability audit, the Beaufort example challenges the belief that such planning and design exercises merely reproduce the status quo. Whereas some plans do minimize change to suit the interests of upper- and middle-income residents, to the detriment of those less well-off, the Beaufort plan specifically encourages, for example, housing diversity and affordability with an emphasis on workforce housing and 'aging in place'. A large segment of work in the case study charrette dealt with substantive issues of housing and quality of life for people of low and moderate incomes.

Overall, the Beaufort case study illustrates how the digital town hall can be used to embed place-based planning information and design codes into the town's e-governance structure. It thus comprises a clear example of Mitchell's thesis that electronic code can give 'character' to a place by encoding rules and protocols that facilitate some activities and discourage others (Mitchell, 1999, p.50). In so doing, these form-based codes become transformed in the virtual realm as 'master codes,' whose articulation of place-based planning and design standards marks a measure of not just 'intelligent' but 'smart' city planning. This particular charrette, with its detailed preparation analyses and subsequent code building methodology, represents state-of-the-art community design practice in the USA. Its extensive scope, its digital presence, the attention to small-scale contextual detail and the creation of market-ready infill and redevelopment projects provide benchmarks of progressive planning practice. In particular, the reciprocal process of designing under a form-based code that is then recalibrated by the site-specific urban design proposals contained in the plan marks a clear advancement of design-based planning in the USA.

In the British context, the localism initiatives promoted by the British Coalition Government in 2010 as a radical overhaul of the national planning system do not yet provide clear guidance on how to meet equivalent challenges to communities in England. Plenty of British cities such as Southampton, Manchester, Newcastle and Edinburgh are making strides towards 'intelligent' and pervasive ICT infrastructures, but the proposed shifts in planning practice raise many unanswered questions regarding ways to ensure that the physical environment of cities, towns and neighbourhoods can be made equivalently smart and sustainable. Form-based and design codes provide one of the most effective means of achieving the kind of location-specific, high-quality design essential as the physical component of smart places, and the American example shows how these concepts should be embedded within the electronic governance structures of towns and cities. However, just as in America, whether or not this combined potential for truly smart communities is utilized to good effect in England may be a political decision rather than a professional one.

NOTES

1   A specific distinction is made in the text between planning in England and the rest of the British Isles. Planning in Wales, Scotland and Northern Ireland follows compatible objectives but is handled with different legislation in the Scottish Parliament and the Welsh and Northern Ireland Assemblies.

2   Form-based codes are an integral component of New Urbanist urban design and planning in the USA. Design codes in England owe much to the American precedent, even while many British architects and urban designers show hostility to New Urbanism. Many mistakenly confuse New Urbanism's urban design concepts and methods with the conservative building aesthetics prevalent in some regions of the States – particularly in the South and in communities along the east coast. New Urbanist developments elsewhere – in California for example – are largely free of these neo-traditional aesthetics, allowing the urban design concepts to be more clearly understood and recognized as parallel to those practiced widely in the UK.

3   For information regarding the timeline of events in Beaufort, the author is indebted to Craig Lewis, principal in The Lawrence Group, Town Planners and Architects, who has led and orchestrated many stages of Beaufort's journey towards a smart and sustainable future.

REFERENCES

Brower, S., 2002, 'The sectors of the transect', *Journal of Urban Design* **7**(3), 313–20.

Carmona, M., Dann, J., 2007a, 'Topic: design codes', *Urban Design* (Quarterly) 101. [available at www.rudi.net/books/15897].

Carmona, M., Dann, J., 2007b, 'Design codes in England, what do we know?', *Urban Design* (Quarterly) 101. www.rudi.net/books/15899.

Castells, M., 1989, *The Informational City: Information Technology, Economic Restructuring and the Urban-Regional Process*, Blackwell, Oxford.

Castells, M., 1997, *The Information Age: Economy, Society, and Culture, 1: The Rise of the Network Society*, Blackwell, Oxford.

Coleman, R., 1978, *Attitudes Towards Neighborhoods: How Americans Choose to Live*. Working Paper No. 49, Joint Center for Urban Studies of MIT and Harvard University, Cambridge, MA.

Conservative Party (UK), 2010, *Policy Green Paper No. 14, Open Source Planning* [www.conservatives.com/~/media/Files/Green%20Papers/planning-greenpaper.ashx].

Congress for the New Urbanism (CNU), 2000, *Charter of the New Urbanism*, McGraw-Hill, New York.

Conzen, M.R.G., 1968, 'The use of town plans in the study of urban history', in H. Dyos (ed), *The Study of Urban History*, St. Martin's Press, New York, 113–30.

Dear, M., 1995, 'Prolegomena to a post modern urbanism', in P. Healey et al. (eds), *Managing Cities: The New Urban Context*, Wiley, London, 27–44.

DETR (Department of the Environment, Transport and the Regions), 2000, *Planning Policy Guidance Note 3: Housing*, DETR, London.

DETR (Department of the Environment, Transport and the Regions) and CABE (Commission for Architecture and the Built Environment), 2000, *By Design: Urban Design in the Planning System: Towards Better Practice*, DETR and CABE, London.

Duany Plater-Zyberk & Company (DPZ), 2002, *The Lexicon of the New Urbanism, Version 3.2.*, FL, DPZ & Co, Miami.

Florida, R., 2002, *The Rise of the Creative Class: And How It's Transforming Work, Leisure, Community and Everyday Life*, Basic Books, New York.

Geddes, P., 1915, *Cities in Evolution*, Williams & Norgate, London, reprinted 1971, *Cities in Evolution: An Introduction to the Town Planning Movement and to the Study of Civics*, Harper & Row, New York.

Gilder, G., 2000, *Telecosm: How Infinite Bandwidth Will Revolutionize Our World*, Free Press, New York.

Graham, S., Marvin, S., 1996, *Telecommunications and the City*, Routledge, London.

Graham, S., Marvin, S., 2001, *Splintering Urbanism*, Routledge, London.

Harvey, D., 1989, *The Condition of Postmodernity: An Enquiry into the Origins of Cultural Change*, Basil Blackwell, Oxford.

Hopkins, R., 2008, *The Transition Handbook: From Oil Dependency to Local Resilience*, Green Books, Totnes.

Howell, P., 1993, 'Public space and the public sphere: political theory and the historical geography of modernity', *Environment and Planning D: Society and Space* **11**, 303–22.

Jameson, F., 1991, *Postmodernism, or, The Cultural Logic of Late Capitalism*, Duke University Press, Durham, NC.

Keane, T., Walters, D., 1995, *Davidson Land Plan*, Town of Davidson, NC.

Kelly, K., 1998, *New Rules for the New Economy: 10 Radical Strategies for a Connected World*, Viking, New York.

Kotkin, J., 2001, 'The new geography of wealth', Reis.com, Techscapes, December.

The Lawrence Group, 2009. *Vision Beaufort 2009 Comprehensive Plan*, The Lawrence Group City of Beaufort, SC.

Lucas, R., 1988, 'On the mechanics of economic development', *Journal of Monetary Economics* **22**, 3–42.

Mitchell, W., 1995, *City of Bits: Space, Place, and the Infobahn*, MIT Press, Cambridge, MA.

Mitchell, W., 1999, *e-Topia: Urban Life, Jim But Not As You Know It*, MIT Press, Cambridge.

Mitchell, W., 2001, 'Equitable access to an on-line world', in D. Schon, B. Sanyal, W. Mitchell (eds), *High Technology and Low-Income Communities*, MIT Press, Cambridge, MA.

ODPM (Office of the Deputy Prime Minister), 2005a, *Delivering Sustainable Development, PPS1*, The Stationery Office, London.

ODPM, 2005b, *Sustainable Communities: People, Places, Prosperity*, The Stationery Office, London.

Parolek, D., Parolek, K., Crawford, P., 2008, *Form-Based Codes: A Guide for Planners, Urban Designers, Municipalities and Developers*, John Wiley & Sons, Inc., Hoboken, NJ.

Pocock, D., Hudson, R., 1978, *Images of the Urban Environment*, MacMillan, London.

Sassen, S., 1991, *The Global City*, 2nd edn, 2002, Princeton University Press, Princeton, NJ.

Sayer, A. 2010, 'Across the pond, a 180-degree turn', *Planning* **76**(10), 14–17.

Sennett, R., 1971, *The Uses of Disorder: Personal Identity and Community Life*, Allen Lane, London.

Sennett, R., 1974, *The Fall of Public Man*, Alfred A. Knopf, New York.

Soja, E., 1989, *Postmodern Geographies*, Verso, London.

Symes, M., Pauwells, S., 1999, 'The diffusion of innovations in urban design: the case of sustainability in the hulme development guide', *Journal of Urban Design* **4**(1), 97–117.

Walters, D., 2007, *Designing Community: Charrettes, Masterplans and Form-based Codes*, Architectural Press, Oxford.

Walters, D., Brown, L., 2004, *Design First: Design-based Planning for Communities*, Architectural Press, Oxford.

Watson, S., Gibson, K. (eds), 1995, *Postmodern Cities and Spaces*, Blackwell, Oxford.

Webber, M.M., 1963. 'Order in diversity: community without propinquity', in: L. Wingo Jr. (ed), *Cities and Space: the Future Use of Urban Land*, Johns Hopkins Press, Baltimore, 25–54.

Webber, M.M., 1964. 'The urban place and the nonplace urban realm', in: M.M. Webber et al. (eds), *Explorations into Urban Structure*, University of Pennsylvania Press, Philadelphia, 19–41.

Index

Page numbers in *Italics* represent tables.
Page numbers in **Bold** represent figures.